# Beatrix Potter
## artist & illustrator

Paintings and drawings selected and introduced by

Anne Stevenson Hobbs

DULWICH PICTURE GALLERY / FREDERICK WARNE

This book was published as the official companion to *Beatrix Potter, Artist and Illustrator,* the exhibition shown at the Dulwich Picture Gallery, London, from 12 October 2005 to 22 January 2006.

FREDERICK WARNE IN ASSOCIATION WITH THE DULWICH PICTURE GALLERY

Published by the Penguin Group
Penguin Books Ltd, 80 Strand, London WC2R 0RL, England
Penguin Group (USA) Inc., 375 Hudson Street, New York, New York 10014, USA
Penguin Group (Canada), 90 Eglinton Avenue East, Suite 700, Toronto, Ontario, Canada M4P 2Y3
Penguin Ireland, 25 St Stephen's Green, Dublin 2, Ireland
Penguin (Group) Australia, 250 Camberwell Road, Camberwell, Victoria 3124, Australia
Penguin Books India (P) Ltd, 11 Community Centre, Panchsheel Park, New Delhi 110 017, India
Penguin Group (NZ), cnr Airborne and Rosedale Roads, Albany, Auckland 1310, New Zealand
Penguin Books (South Africa) (Pty) Ltd, P O Box 9, Parklands 2121, South Africa

Penguin Books Ltd, Registered Offices: 80 Strand, London WC2R 0RL, England

Web site at: www.peterrabbit.com

First published by Frederick Warne 2005
10 9 8 7 6 5 4 3 2 1



ISBN 0 7232 5700 0

Design by Perfect Bound

Printed and bound in China

# Foreword

Ian A C Dejardin
*Director, Dulwich Picture Gallery*

I was fortunate enough to live for some years in the Lake District, not so far from Far Sawrey, where Beatrix Potter had lived. She, like another local lady of an earlier era, Lady Anne Clifford, seemed to have somehow imprinted herself on the collective memory of the place. Stories were still told of 'Mrs. Heelis's' (never 'Beatrix Potter's') acuity at the sheep market; her eye for a good Herdwick sheep was legendary. It was – almost – as if she were still alive. And, of course, in one way she is genuinely immortal – because her famous books are still loved and read and admired, part of everyone's childhood. Peter Rabbit, Squirrel Nutkin, Benjamin Bunny, Mrs. Tiggy-winkle and the rest have entered the language, both verbally and visually. While many illustrators have occasionally tried their hand, with some success, at writing their own text – E.H. Shepard and Heath Robinson both did it – only Potter is as famous for her words as for her images. But like those artists, and Arthur Rackham, another famous illustrator whose work has been featured in an exhibition here at Dulwich Picture Gallery, there is much more to Beatrix Potter's talent than the characters who made her famous. Anne Stevenson Hobbs, curator of the show, has put together an exhaustive demonstration of the many facets of Potter's skill. There is Potter the landscapist, Potter the scientific observer, Potter the unrivalled recorder of the natural world, alongside Potter the storyteller and illustrator. She was a draughtsman and watercolourist of astonishing skill, by any standards. The exhibition will be a revelation to many a fan of Peter Rabbit.

This project could never have got off the ground without the exceptional expertise of the show's curator and author of the catalogue, Anne Stevenson Hobbs, who was, until her retirement in 2002, the Frederick Warne Curator of Children's Literature at the Victoria and Albert Museum. Her knowledge of the V&A's remarkable collections has been invaluable, and we are particularly grateful to Anne's former employers as spectacularly generous lenders – our thanks to Mark Jones, Director, to Susan Lambert, the (then) Keeper of Word and Image, and to her successor, Julius Bryant. Private lenders show a special kind of generosity in lending: we owe them all our sincere thanks for allowing us to deprive them of their treasured possessions for a short time.

We are especially grateful to Liz Hunter (The National Trust), Michelle Kelly (The Armitt), Emma Laws (V&A Museum), Karen Lightner (Free Library of Philadelphia), and Sara Mills (Frederick Warne). Anne Stevenson Hobbs would also like to thank the following for their invaluable help: Elizabeth Battrick, John Cawood, Brigadier John Heelis, Professor Linda Lear, Colin Liddie, Lolly Robinson, Judy Taylor Hough and Michael Wright.

At Dulwich Picture Gallery the exhibition has been expertly organised by Vicky Norton and her team, Eloise Stewart, James Hall and Mella Shaw, to the latter of whom fell much of the administrative burden on this occasion. Steven Atherton and Jack Kettlewell led the installation team; and the whole project has been ably supported by Kate Knowles, Head of Marketing and Publicity, and Dida Tait, Head of Development.

Final mention must go to our very happy collaboration with Frederick Warne & Co. Ltd, Beatrix Potter's own publishers, and the publishers of this book, who gave active and enthusiastic support right from the outset.

## NOTES AND SOURCES

### PAGE NUMBERS OF BEATRIX POTTER'S BOOKS

These refer to the 2002 editions of the 'little books', the 1985 edition of *The Fairy Caravan* (reprinted in paperback 1992) and the 1930 US edition of *The Tale of Little Pig Robinson.*

### ILLUSTRATIONS

If a drawing is coloured, this is indicated at the start of the description; the order of the description does not necessarily follow the order in which a drawing was executed.

'Sepia' is the term generally used to refer to brown ink.

### KEY TO ABBREVIATIONS OF SOURCES

AT The Armitt Trust
BPS Beatrix Potter Society
FLP Free Library of Philadelphia
FW Frederick Warne & Co.
NPG National Portrait Gallery
NT The National Trust
PC Private collection
V&A Victoria and Albert Museum
WA Frederick Warne Archive

# Contents


| | |
|---|---|
| INTRODUCTION | 6 |
| TIMELINE | 10 |
| PORTRAITS | 14 |
| NATURAL HISTORY AND ARTEFACTS | 23 |
| Fauna | 24 |
| Flora | 44 |
| Fungi | 48 |
| Fossils | 56 |
| Artefacts | 57 |
| THE YOUNG ARTIST | 59 |
| Family background and early work | 59 |
| First published work | 74 |
| Fantasy and humour | 81 |
| ILLUSTRATIONS | 86 |
| NARRATIVE SEQUENCES | 92 |
| THE BOOKS AND THEIR BACKGROUNDS | 100 |
| The little books | 100 |
| The rhyme books | 118 |
| Sawrey books | 130 |
| Book design | 135 |
| LATER LIFE AND WORK | 140 |
| Farming and domestic life | 141 |
| The Fairy Caravan | 151 |
| Buildings, landscapes and gardens | 156 |
| The Tale of Little Pig Robinson | 170 |
| Tributes | 174 |
| The 'little side shows' | 181 |
| Collections and Illustration Acknowledgements | 185 |
| Bibliography | 186 |
| Index | 187 |

# Introduction

**Repetition and variety, the keynotes of nature,** are also the keynotes of Beatrix Potter's art, especially outside the 'little books' which have overshadowed her other achievements. Repetition, because she continually returned to favourite themes, redrawing and recopying, endlessly attempting to capture the world about her; variety, because within her own limits that range of subjects and styles was as wide as her experience allowed.

'It is all the same, drawing, painting, modelling, the irresistible desire to copy any beautiful object which strikes the eye. Why cannot one be content to look at it? I cannot rest, I must draw, however poor the result . . .' Through constant practice and experiment, and a relentless striving for perfection ('I "polish! polish! polish!" – to the last revise . . .'), she rose to a high level of competence, both in her distinguished achievement as an illustrator of natural history and in the little books that began almost by accident.

Expression and imagination matured sooner in her words than in her pictures. In the coded Journal kept from her mid-teens until the age of thirty-one, she recorded vivid and visual impressions of places, people and animals, scraps of gossip, social comment, and some robust observations on art ('No one will read this'). She never passively accepted the general view. Maurice Sendak has described the Journal as 'an enormous sketchbook in which she tried to teach herself how to see and write'.

Just as Potter practised writing in her Journal, so in her drawings she was 'trying to copy nature – without affectation or swelled head'. 'I can't invent: I only copy,' she was to claim, yet 'nothing could be more invented' (Banner, 1946). Potter never aped another artist's manner, but continued to 'copy what she saw' according to her creed. 'What we call highest and lowest in nature are both equally perfect' – here she echoes the Aesthetes – from the swill bucket to the Lakeland hills whose watery atmosphere had captivated so many artists before her. To her exacting eye, very few landscape artists saw the 'beauty of nature unadorned'. Whatever the subject, she tackled it with professional detachment: 'I see no reason why common-sense should not foster a healthier appreciation of beauty than morbid sentimentality.'

'It sometimes happens that the town child is more alive to the fresh beauty of the country than a child who is country born.' Alert and curious about the world, Beatrix and her younger brother Bertram, who shared her enthusiasms, found inspiration during holiday escapes from London, her 'unloved birthplace', especially to Scotland or, from 1882, the Lake District. The earliest drawing books include flowers and rabbits, buildings and landscapes; they reappear in her Tales. Trees in particular intrigued her both scientifically and imaginatively. So many professional woodland landscape painters had never considered 'how the branches grow from a tree trunk', she wrote to Delmar Banner in 1937. Trees 'are *in the right place* – as beautiful as rocks. And they have a nobility of growth which is usually intirely [*sic*] over looked.' Advising a young illustrator some years earlier, she remarked: 'I did so many careful botanical studies in my youth, it became easy for me to draw twigs. And little details like that add to the reality of a picture.' The fossil studies and archaeological paintings, exquisite in drawing and composition, rank with her best work, the paintings of fungi. Frederick Walker, Birket Foster and William Henry Hunt had seen the fascination in fungi, but no botanical painter of her time or since has been able to equal her rendering of their shape, colour and texture.

▷ **Beatrix Potter, by Delmar Banner**
***1938***
Beatrix Potter first met the young artists Delmar and Josefina Banner at Eskdale Show. Keswick Show is the setting for this portrait of 'a bonny lady', in her best Herdwick tweed coat. She holds the umbrella which had belonged to Norman Warne, her first fiancé, who died eight years before her marriage to William Heelis.

The distinguished sculptor Josefina de Vasconcellos (b. 1904) became a close friend of Beatrix Potter, who affectionately nicknamed her 'Pigwig'. Echoing Constable, Potter offered practical criticism of Delmar Banner's pictures: 'Your husband has learnt clouds. Light next please. He has the *drawing* which is the foundation.'
*Oil on canvas*
*749x622mm*
NPG

Associated in the public imagination with one style, Potter experimented with medium, technique and scale. The 'miniaturist' painted spiders and mushrooms ten times larger than her vignettes. The practitioner of naturalism and precise detail played with broad washes and a palette of bright primaries. The discipline of the camera and the microscope guided her vision, but she had, in her own words, the 'seeing eye' and a 'peculiarly precocious and tenacious memory': both for places and for the sentiments they evoked.

All her life, observation inspired experimentation, perhaps because she had 'an open mind, not in a groove'. She could look at similar subjects in different ways and tackle them in a variety of styles and techniques. Back in the schoolroom, she had tried everything from transfer printing to etching, and took naturally to modelling. At the age of eighteen she was producing bold chalk drawings, and, in complete contrast, a number of rather static studies in pen and ink, fine-grained and crosshatched. Having explored the versatility of pencil, pen and crayon, she went on to discover the sculptural possibilities of monochrome 'grisaille' wash, a technique that briefly coexists with the even smaller dry-pigment brushstrokes of her miniaturist watercolours. This *pointilliste* stipple method made possible a virtuoso rendering of bloom and texture. Here she was influenced, as she admitted, by the Pre-Raphaelites, and 'their somewhat niggling but absolutely genuine admiration for copying natural details'. Her definition of the myopic intensity of Pre-Raphaelite painting is an extraordinarily perceptive one: an absence of shadow, and 'everything in focus at once, which though natural in the different planes of the picture, produces on the whole a different impression from that which we receive from nature'.

Emulating Randolph Caldecott, the only artist she 'really tried to copy', she soon began to adopt a broader sweep, with a bolder, more fluid 'sepia' line in pliable quill pen or brush and a wash in clean fresh colours. (The muted tints of her early greetings cards had been dictated by the demands of chromolithography.) Denser, darker hues convey dead blackbird and furry spider, and vivid multi-coloured brushstrokes the gleaming prickles of a hedgehog: an experiment extended for sheep heads in a later, looser pointillism and yet brighter palette, an adventurous style that few would associate with 'Beatrix Potter'. The smiling landscapes of her Tales label her as a 'fair-weather painter', like Helen Allingham; but shadowy nocturnes, moon- or candle-lit, suggest oppression and even nightmare: a long panelled corridor, a wood from fairy tale. Most of the later sketches, painted at speed in blobs of melting wash, were done in autumn damps and winter snow. Some atmospheric effects, not unlike Ruskin's cloud formations, are a reminder of her lifelong respect for Turner. Other landscapes, daringly impressionistic and almost abstract, recall the late Wilson Steer. Quick sketches tend to look avant-garde in comparison with finished work; even so, these studies seem startlingly modern. Amateurs are usually behind the times, and make little progress through their careers – but Potter was no amateur. As she remarked to Delmar Banner, perhaps thinking of her own work: artists move on, leaving behind the 'topographically-exact-in-detail' stage. Her mature diversity of styles came not so much from deteriorating eyesight as from a changing inner vision.

Colour work was becoming an effort; Potter blamed her tired eyes on close work at the microscope. Many of her last paintings – *Peter Rabbit* recopied to make money for the preservation of Windermere, some colour plates for the late books – are sadly garish or smudgy. But the pen-and-inks done in her sixties are as accomplished as any of her line work.

Beatrix Potter never 'cared tuppence' for popularity, yet in 1920 she wrote, 'It seems a pity ... that some of my old miscellaneous drawings cannot be published, as several people have remarked.' At least six hundred of those 'miscellaneous drawings' are scientific studies. Only a handful include people: human intrusion is avoided. Potter found human anatomy 'a terrible bother', but the handful of dashed-off figures in her sketchbooks and the stick people of her picture letters are full of life. Nearly all the figures in her landscapes are animals, an intrinsic part of their settings. The scenery is much more than a backdrop; her skilfully placed figures need their settings more than the landscapes need figures.

Even in the nursery, Beatrix observed the behaviour of her pet animals as well as their anatomy. She learned the structure of bone and muscle; she knew their resting and running positions, their hibernating and breathing patterns, and was well equipped to draw them in all their grace and power. The fifteen years between late adolescence and her early thirties were a time of intensive and painstaking apprenticeship, but her imagination had only temporarily gone underground. Scientific studies metamorphosed into imagined characters, and an irrepressible lava of humour bubbled through, in both Journal and drawings. The lively wit of her first public art, the 1890 greetings cards, was nothing new. Rabbits inspired an exceptional number of drawings, but mice populate the early rhyme pictures: dancing, spinning, or stealing. The invertebrates and insects, amphibians and reptiles provide supporting cast and local colour: a snail on the wall, a fly on the doll's house roof, a whole *corps de ballet* in *The Tale of Mrs. Tittlemouse*.

The settings are seen from an animal's perspective, but in her scaled-down world Potter contrives to make oblique satirical comments on society. Human beings reminded her of animals, and the Journal is sprinkled with devastating cameos: 'How amusing Aunt Harriet is, she is more like a weasel than ever.' She confessed that a few of her imaginary creatures were 'harmless skits' or caricatures, but they behave in character, and she draws them with knowledge, affection and respect. The body-language may be half-human; the bodies are not.

Parody seemed irresistible – verbal or visual, conscious or unconscious, but usually tongue-in-cheek and concealed. Peter Rabbit at the closed door is a sly reflection of someone else's painting. Potter pays homage to Hogarth, in *The Tailor of Gloucester*, and to Tenniel, to Caldecott and Lear. Jemima Puddle-duck, with updated bonnet and shawl, has waddled straight out of a German folk-tale illustration by Speckter. Some commentators lay on Potter's pictures a greater burden than they can possibly bear, yet fail to notice their hidden parody. She challenges us to discover her private jokes.

In the natural history paintings such subterfuge has no place. The subjects themselves challenge the artist to paint their portraits. Ever volatile, they are caught mid-scamper, or just about to spring. In convenient repose, they seem even more arresting: minute spiders, deceptively enlarged by the microscope; skulls, glazed and sightless but equally emphatic; the roe-deer's mask; and the tragic stag, sprawled in the abandon of death. Newly

▷ **Waterlilies**
*[ca. 1903?]*
*Watercolour, ink wash, black ink and Indian ink*
*227x291mm*
LT

dead, long since stuffed, or just resting, Potter's animals have as glossy a presence as her fungi, which celebrate new life born from decay. The fungi seem almost alive. They nestle semi-camouflaged among pine-needles and leaves, squat in lichen and moss, or are profiled among stiff grasses, in the tradition of Dürer's *The Great Piece of Turf.*

She makes one see, smell and touch what she paints, and has a sensuous awareness of the texture and solidity of each object: crumbling leather and flaking rust, the papery rustle of onion skins, the stiffness of a small dead fish with its accusing gelatinous eye. She describes subtle differences in plumage or fur, and the infinite gradations from light to dark. A dash of colour may act as a focal point, sometimes doubling as light source (a candle, an open doorway, a glowing hearth). Moonlight reflected on swirling water, dusty sunbeams slanting into a cellar, the play of light through bay leaves or translucent ears – all are instances of her fascination with the effects of light and shade.

Potter had a strong sense of pictorial composition, and definite ideas about the relationship of picture to text; she liked to dictate the layout of her books. The viewpoint can be an unconventional one. Parts of the picture dash off the page; centrifugal movement is accelerated when a peaceful clustering of mice turns into scurrying mayhem. Round or oval vignettes set off the forms they enclose – a fireplace or a hollow forest glade. A rising or receding, zigzagging spiral increases the sense of recession and depth and leads the eye upwards, 'over the hills and far away'.

She sometimes feels the need to 'improve' the composition – compressing what she sees, or modifying it to create a composite view, bending the rules of naturalism and the arrangements of geology. Apart from such occasional leanings to the Picturesque, Potter's places are real rather than ideal. Her true affinity was to the Lake District.

Following the nostalgia of her time for roots and rusticity, she became drawn to North Country vernacular. In these snug cottage kitchens, conviviality seems in preparation if not in progress. It is a temporary safety only, as signalled by the alert ears and the little wild eyes. Outside is a decidedly uncosy world of murderous gardeners, foxes and wolves.

'What she instinctively felt about spaces – that they should be comforting, responsive and protective – was part of a general realization about spaces common to artists,' writes Alison Smithson; Beatrix Potter 'succeeded in portraying forms entirely suitable for their purpose.' Smithson seems to echo the twenty-eight-year-old Potter. Good design, and 'that appreciation of the fitness of things which is the soul of artistic taste', were important to her in all the arts – in elegant costume, china or chairs. Equally suited to its purpose, and inseparable from its landscape, is the indigenous architecture of the Lake District, which became part of the fabric of her books.

The rational approach, the naturalism and nostalgia, the pastorals and the sense of place, the preference for watercolour, the interest in detail and narrative – all are manifestations of Beatrix Potter's essential Englishness. As artist-storyteller, she was one of a rare breed. Peculiarly her own are the energy and wit, the sense of movement and vigorous life. Through a subtle combination of composition, light and colour, more senses than sight are stimulated – the feel of smooth slate or dry leaves, the taste and smell of fog and frost, the unheard airs that accompany her dancing line.

# Timeline

## Compiled by Judy Taylor

**1866** *July 28* Helen Beatrix Potter born at 2 Bolton Gardens, South Kensington, London, first child of Helen and Rupert Potter.

**1871** Potter family holiday at Dalguise House, Dunkeld, Scotland, their 'summer home' for the next eleven years.

**1872** *March 14* Walter Bertram Potter, Beatrix's brother, born at 2 Bolton Gardens.

**1875** Earliest example of Beatrix's drawing, a sketchbook at age nine, of birds, butterflies and caterpillars (Victoria & Albert Museum, London).

**1880** *April 22* Art Student's Certificate, Science and Art Department, South Kensington, for model drawing and freehand. 'Excellent' in both.

**1881** First entry in fifteen-year-old Beatrix's Journal in a code devised by her; simple letter-for-letter substitution not 'cracked' until 1958.

*May 6* Art Student's Certificate for practical geometry and perspective. Again 'excellent' in both categories.

**1882** *July–October* Potter family's first Lake District holiday, at Wray Castle. Beatrix meets Hardwicke Rawnsley, one of the three founders of the National Trust.

**1883** *April 18* Miss Annie Carter, aged nineteen, appointed as new governess and German teacher for sixteen-year-old Beatrix.

*April 19* Eleven-year-old Bertram sent away to boarding school.

**1884** *January 31* Earliest known example of Beatrix's drawing of bats (Victoria & Albert Museum). She was seventeen.

**1885** Annie Carter leaves the Potter household to marry Edwin Moore.

Beatrix acquires a rabbit, Benjamin Bouncer.

**1886** *February* Beatrix's first recorded microscope watercolour – study of gnat's leg (Victoria & Albert Museum).

**1887** *April–May* Beatrix has serious rheumatic fever affecting her heart.

*October 12* Beatrix's earliest recorded fungus drawing, Verdigris Toadstool (*Stropharia aeruginosa*) (Armitt).

*December 24* Birth of Moores' first child, Noël Christian.

**1889** Benjamin Bouncer models for Potter family Christmas cards.

**1890** *May 14* Beatrix sells first drawings to Hildesheimer & Faulkner, London. Used as greetings cards and illustrations to book of rhymes, *A Happy Pair* by Frederic E. Weatherly.

**1891** *November 10* Potters put Camfield Place on the market, Beatrix's paternal grandparents' house since 1866.

*November 12* Beatrix's sketches are rejected by Frederick Warne.

**1892** *October 29* In Birnam, Scotland, Beatrix meets Charles McIntosh, the 'Perthshire Naturalist', to discuss her paintings of fungi and mosses. He sends specimens of fungi to London for her to paint.

Publishers Ernest Nister buy Beatrix's drawings to illustrate children's annuals.

**1893** *September 3* At Eastwood, Dunkeld, Scotland, Beatrix paints the rare fungus Old Man of the Woods (*Strobilomyces floccopus*) (Armitt and Perth Museum).

*September 4* From Eastwood, Dunkeld, Beatrix sends five-year-old Noël Moore a story about her pet rabbit, Peter.

*September 5* Beatrix sends four-year-old Eric Moore a picture letter about 'a frog called Mr. Jeremy Fisher'.

**1894** *January 10* Charles McIntosh suggests Beatrix includes technical points in her fungus paintings 'to make them more perfect as botanical drawings'.

*June 12* Beatrix visits her cousin, Caroline Hutton, at Harescombe Grange, near Stroud, in Gloucestershire, noting, 'I had not been away independently for five years.'

*July 17–early October* In Lennel, Scotland, Beatrix draws the important botanical fossil *Araucarioxylon*, now *Pitus*.

*October* Beatrix records in her Journal that 'more or less in a year' she had learned by heart six complete plays by Shakespeare.

*October* Beatrix draws to scale a collection of Roman objects found in the City of London 1872-73.

**1895** *March* Ernest Nister publish Beatrix's drawings 'A Frog he would a-fishing go' in *Nister's Holiday Annual for 1896* and in *Comical Customers at the New Stores of Comical Rhymes and Stories*.

Caroline Martineau commissions Beatrix to prepare twelve

◁ **Young Beatrix, photographed by her father**
BPS
▷ **Beatrix, her father, brother Bertram and mother, with the dog Spot in the foreground, ca. 1881**
V&A
▷▷**Noël Moore, the first reader of *The Tale of Peter Rabbit***
PC

lithographed plates of insects. Only the Sheet Web Spider and the Privet Hawk Moth survive. It is not known if remaining ten were ever finished.

**1896** *May 20* Beatrix to Royal Botanic Gardens, Kew, with her uncle, Sir Henry Roscoe, to show her fungus drawings to Director William Thiselton-Dyer.

*July 15–October 6* Potters holiday in Near Sawrey in the Lake District, Beatrix commenting, 'It is as nearly perfect a little place as I ever lived in.'

*December 7* Beatrix delivers Paper on germination of fungus spores to Thiselton-Dyer and is rejected.

**1897** *January 31* Final entry in Journal notes Beatrix is hard at work revising her Paper, 'On the Germination of the Spores of *Agaricineae*'.

*April 1* Paper by thirty-year-old Helen B. Potter presented to the Linnean Society of London by George Massee from Kew, women not being allowed to attend Society meetings.

**1901** *January 26* Peter Rabbit dies. Beatrix later wrote, 'Whatever the limitations of his intellect or outward shortcomings of his fur, and his ears and toes, his disposition was uniformly amiable and his temper unfailingly sweet. An affectionate companion and a quiet friend.'

*September 18* Frederick Warne show interest in *The Tale of Peter Rabbit and Mr. McGregor's Garden* by Beatrix Potter but reject rhyming text by Hardwicke Rawnsley. Beatrix refuses to colour her black-and-white illustrations.

*September 25* Beatrix tells story of Squirrel Nutkin in picture letter to eight-year-old Norah Moore.

*December 16* Beatrix publishes 250 copies of *The Tale of Peter Rabbit* privately, with black-and-white illustrations and coloured frontispiece.

**1902** *February* Beatrix reprints 200 copies of *The Tale of Peter Rabbit*.

*July* Beatrix plans book of rhymes called *Appley Dapply*, an abridged edition of which would not be published until 1917.

*October* Frederick Warne publish 8,000 copies of *The Tale of Peter Rabbit*, shortened and illustrated in full colour throughout.

*November 20* Bertram Potter secretly married to Mary Welsh Scott in Edinburgh.

*December* Beatrix privately publishes 500 copies of *The Tailor of Gloucester*.

**1903** *August* *The Tale of Squirrel Nutkin* is published by Frederick Warne.

*October* A shorter version of *The Tailor of Gloucester* published by Warne.

*November 26–December 3* Beatrix, on holiday in Hastings, writes *The Tale of Two Bad Mice*, *The Tale of Tuppenny*, and *The Pie and the Patty-Pan*.

*December 28* Beatrix registers her Peter Rabbit doll at the Patent Office.

**1904** *September* *The Tale of Benjamin Bunny* and *The Tale of Two Bad Mice* published by Warne.

*December 7* Beatrix sends Warne the plan and rules for *The Game of Peter Rabbit*.

**1905** *July 25* Beatrix receives written proposal of marriage from her editor, Norman Warne. Against her parents' wishes, thirty-nine-year-old Beatrix accepts.

*August 25* Norman Warne dies of leukaemia, aged thirty-seven.

Peter Rabbit wallpaper goes on sale.

*September* *The Tale of Mrs. Tiggy-Winkle* published by Warne.

*October* *The Pie and the Patty-Pan* published by Warne, first of series in larger format and first with black-and-white illustrations as well as colour plates.

*November* Beatrix buys Hill Top, a working farm in Near Sawrey.

**1906** *July* *The Tale of Mr. Jeremy Fisher* published by Warne in original 'little book' format.

*September* Beatrix starts to breed Herdwick sheep at Hill Top Farm.

*November* *The Story of Miss Moppet* and *The Story of a Fierce Bad Rabbit* published in panoramic format by Warne.

**1907** Beatrix visits Hill Top Farm whenever she can get away from London. She now has cows, ducks, hens and pigs, as well as sheep.

*September* *The Tale of Tom Kitten* published by Warne.

**1908** *August* *The Tale of Jemima Puddle-Duck* published by Warne.

◁◁ **Beatrix in the porch of Hill Top in 1913, the year of her marriage to William Heelis**
NT

◁ **Anne Carroll Moore, from the New York Public Library, who visited Beatrix in 1921**
New York Public Library

*October* *The Roly-Poly Pudding* published by Warne in larger format.

**1909** Beatrix buys second farm in Near Sawrey, Castle Farm.

*July* *The Tale of the Flopsy Bunnies*, sequel to *Peter Rabbit* and *Benjamin Bunny*, published by Warne.

*October* *Ginger and Pickles* published by Warne in larger format.

**1910** *June 17* Beatrix registers Jemima Puddle-Duck doll at the Patent Office.

*July* *The Tale of Mrs. Tittlemouse* published by Warne.

**1911** *October* *The Tale of Timmy Tiptoes* and *Peter Rabbit's Painting Book* published by Warne.

**1912** *October* *The Tale of Mr. Tod* published by Warne, advertised as 'The Peter Rabbit Books, Series II, New Style'.

Beatrix successfully campaigns against hydroplanes on Windermere.

*End of year* Forty-six-year-old Beatrix accepts proposal of marriage from Lake District solicitor, William Heelis.

**1913** *October* *The Tale of Pigling Bland* published by Warne.

*October 15* Beatrix Potter and William Heelis marry at St Mary Abbots', Kensington, London. Choose Castle Cottage as their home, keeping Hill Top as a place for Beatrix to work.

**1914** *May 8* Beatrix's father, Rupert Potter, dies in London, aged eighty-two.

*August 4* Britain declares war on Germany. Beatrix manages the farms, feeding the calves, pigs and poultry.

**1916** *April* Eleanor (Louie) Choyce, aged forty, is employed by Beatrix to help with the farm and garden.

*October* *The Story of Miss Moppet* and *The Story of a Fierce Bad Rabbit* issued by Warne in 'little books' format.

**1917** *April 26* Harold Warne sentenced to eighteen months' imprisonment for forgeries.

*June* Frederick Warne, in serious financial trouble, ask Beatrix for a new book.

*October* Warne publish *Appley Dapply's Nursery Rhymes*, the collection of rhymes begun in 1902.

*May* Peter Rabbit handkerchiefs go on sale.

*June 22* Bertram Potter dies at home in Scotland, of a cerebral haemorrhage, aged forty-six.

*November 11* Armistice signed between the Allies and Germany, marking end of First World War.

*December* *The Tale of Johnny Town-Mouse* published by Warne.

**1919** *May 25* New firm, Frederick Warne & Company Limited, registered in London.

Beatrix buys Lindeth How, Windermere, for eighty-year-old Helen Potter.

Helps to set up Nursing Trust for villages of Sawrey, Hawkshead and Wray; buys house and car for nurse.

**1920** *May 28* Canon Hardwicke Rawnsley dies, aged sixty-nine.

**1921** *May* *The Tale of Peter Rabbit* and *The Tale of Benjamin Bunny* published in French by Warne, as *Pierre Lapin* and *Jeannot Lapin*.

Six of the 'little books' published in Braille by the Royal Institute for the Blind.

*June 27* Anne Carroll Moore, Superintendent of Children's Work, New York Public Library, visits Beatrix and encourages her to write a new book.

*December* *Cecily Parsley's Nursery Rhymes* published by Warne.

**1923** Beatrix buys Troutbeck Park Farm, 1,900-acre sheep farm.

Potter family home in London, 2 Bolton Gardens, sold.

**1925** *August* *Jemima Puddle-Duck's Painting Book* published by Warne.

**1926** *October* Title of *The Roly-Poly Pudding* changed to *The Tale of Samuel Whiskers* and reprinted in 'little book' format. The title not changed in USA until 1980s.

*November* Beatrix employs shepherd Tom Storey at Troutbeck Park Farm.

Tom Storey moves from Troutbeck Park to Hill Top Farm.

*May* Beatrix sells fifty redrawn Peter Rabbit illustrations through *The Horn Book Magazine*, Boston, for the National Trust to save the Windermere lake frontage from developers.

▷ **Award-winning Herdwick ewe with her shepherd, Tom Storey, and her owner, Beatrix Potter, 1930**
NT

▷▷ **Beatrix with her Pekes, Tzusee and Chuleh in 1936**
PC

*September 21* Thirteen-year-old Henry P. Coolidge from Boston visits Beatrix. *The Fairy Caravan* would be dedicated to him.

**1928** *September* Warne publish *Peter Rabbit's Almanac for 1929*.

**1929** *October* David McKay, Philadelphia, publish *The Fairy Caravan*, not available in UK until July 1952.

**1930** *January 31* Sixty-three-year-old Beatrix buys 5,000-acre Monk Coniston Estate on condition that National Trust will take over half when money raised.

*September* Beatrix wins silver challenge cup for best Lake District Herdwick ewe.

*September* *The Tale of Little Pig Robinson* published by Frederick Warne and David McKay. USA edition has more illustrations.

*October* Half Monk Coniston Estate bought by National Trust from Beatrix, who agrees to continue management of entire estate.

**1931** *December* Beatrix starts new book, intended as sequel to *The Fairy Caravan*.

**1932** *December* David McKay publish *Sister Anne*, 'an absurd and grisly version of *Bluebeard*', illustrated by Katharine Sturges. Never issued in the UK.

*December 20* Helen Potter dies aged ninety-three.

**1936** *March* Approaching seventy, Beatrix acquires first Pekinese dog, Tzusee.

Walt Disney's request to make film of *Peter Rabbit* refused by Beatrix. 'To enlarge…will show up all the imperfections.'

*July* Beatrix buys second Pekinese puppy, Chuleh.

*July* Noël Moore, 'a middle aged active man, a clergyman in Kent', visits Beatrix at Hill Top.

**1937** *January 1* Beatrix hands over management of National Trust half of Monk Coniston Estate to their first Lake District Land Agent, Bruce Thompson.

**1938** *July 13* Beatrix agrees to Braille edition of *The Fairy Caravan* in USA.

*November* Beatrix has operation in the Women's Hospital, Liverpool.

**1939** *March 30* In hospital again, Beatrix dictates her Will and asks close friends to look after her husband 'if I don't return'.

*April* Beatrix returns to Castle Cottage to convalesce.

*July 3* Watches sheep-shearing and cattle-herding at Troutbeck Park Farm.

*September 3* Britain and France declare war on Germany.

*October* Beatrix and William buy pony cart to help stretch petrol ration.

Beatrix supervises farm work and breeds rabbits to supplement meat ration. Willie serves on War Agricultural Committee and as reserve policeman.

**1941** *April* Whole edition of *The Tale of Peter Rabbit* lost in bombing raid on London.

*April 19* Warne send Beatrix original *Peter Rabbit* drawings for safekeeping.

*May* Louie Choyce returns to Hill Top to help on the farm.

*December 7* Japanese bomb Pearl Harbor, Hawaii.

*December 8* Britain and USA declare war on Japan.

**1942** *January* Beatrix receives first food parcel from friends in USA.

**1943** *March 19* At AGM of Herdwick Sheep Breeders' Association Beatrix elected President from March 1944. She would have been first woman President of the Association.

*August* Beatrix agrees to publication of *Wag-by-Wall* (story originally intended for *The Fairy Caravan*) in Christmas edition of *The Horn Book Magazine*, then agrees to postponement until May for Twentieth Anniversary Issue. She would not live to see publication.

*December 10* Beatrix struck down by bronchitis and heart trouble.

*December 22* Seventy-seven-year-old Beatrix Potter Heelis dies in the night at Castle Cottage, her husband by her side.

Cremated in Blackpool, Beatrix's ashes scattered by her shepherd and farm manager, Tom Storey, on her land in Near Sawrey.

**1945** *August 4* William Heelis dies in Parey Crost Nursing Home, York. The joint Heelis property, over 4,000 acres with seventeen farms and eight cottages, bequeathed to National Trust.

# PORTRAITS

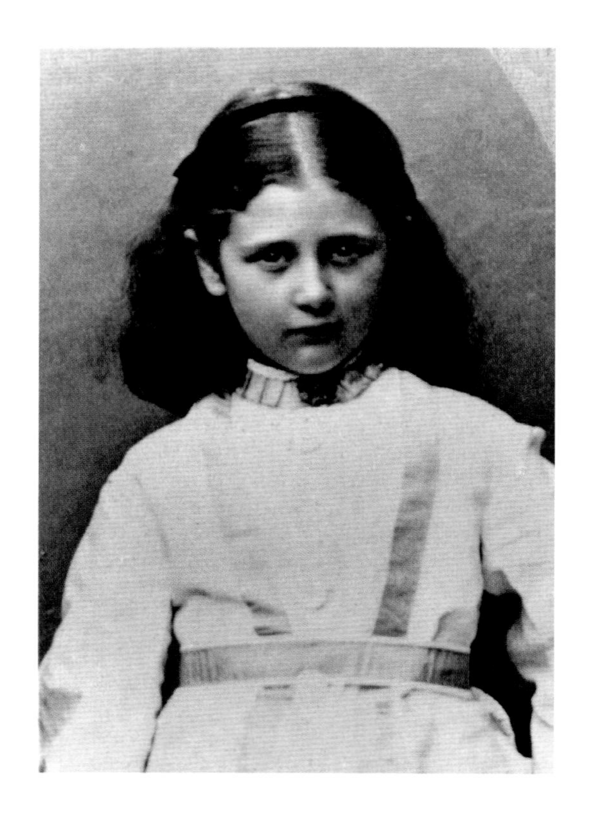

◁ **Beatrix, with black velvet hairband**
*[1871-1872]*
Enlarged detail from a group photograph by Rupert Potter, in which Beatrix is flanked by two female relations. She later recalled her 'absurdly uncomfortable ... white piqué starched frocks just like Tenniel's Alice in Wonderland', and the black velvet hairband that she wore on Sundays.
*Photograph: gelatin silver bromide print*
*176x122mm*
V&A (Linder Bequest)

▷ **Beatrix Potter and Mr. Gaskell at Dalguise**
*[1870-1871]*
William Gaskell, Unitarian minister and widower of the novelist Elizabeth Gaskell, was a close friend of Beatrix Potter's paternal grandparents and a regular guest during their late summer holidays in Scotland; the connection continued after Edmund Potter's death. Remembering his gentle smile, Beatrix wrote: 'There has always been a deep child-like affection between him and me.'
*Photoprint made from a glass negative, copied from an original by Rupert Potter*
BPS

## Rupert Potter and photography

Beatrix Potter inherited her artistic talents especially from her father, who was a competent draughtsman and a distinguished amateur photographer. 'Mr. Millais says the professionals aren't fit to hold a candle to papa.' Rupert Potter was on intimate terms with Millais as probably no other photographer was with an artist of such high reputation (M. Harvey). Potter supplied him with landscape backgrounds and portraits of models, as well as photographs of paintings in progress. The *Pall Mall Gazette*, in its memorial tribute to the orator and statesman John Bright, advertised for sale a set of Rupert Potter's photographs illustrating Mr. Bright's life in the Highlands, and several are included in *The Life and Letters of Sir John Everett Millais* (1899).

Beatrix herself explored and experimented with the medium. It influenced her sense of composition, and she became an accomplished practitioner, recording places and people as well as fossils and fungi, and using photographs as an aid to painting.

Rupert Potter was proud of his daughter and her books, and used to present friends with inscribed copies. Sending one by post, he wrote: 'I think I am rather proud of my daughter's freshness of humour which has never yet become dull.'

△ **Beatrix Potter at the age of ten**
*[1876]*
Striking in these early portraits is the sitter's penetrating and watchful gaze.
*Photograph: gelatin silver bromide print*
*183x138mm*
V&A (Linder Bequest)

◁ **The young Beatrix**
*[ca. 1872?]*
Like the portrait of Beatrix with Mr. Gaskell, this is one of a collection of photographs copied from an unknown source by Leslie Linder, the pioneering student of Potter's work and decoder of her Journal.
*Photoprint made from a glass negative, copied from an original by Rupert Potter*
BPS

▷ **Beatrix and the spaniel Spot**
*1880*
Spot, a constant companion from 1879 until his death in April 1892, appears in many photographs and a few drawings. Beatrix wears an embroidered apron and an asymmetrically buttoned coat like Brer Fox in her illustration to *Uncle Remus*.
*Photograph: albumen print (gold tinted)*
*114x84mm*
V&A (Linder Bequest)

◁ **Beatrix at the age of fifteen, with Spot**
***[1881]***
Taken in the doorway of Dalguise House, Perthshire, a favourite background for photographs, individual or grouped, of family and friends.

Between 1870 and 1894 the family spent fourteen summers – nearly four years of Beatrix Potter's life – on holiday in Scotland, where her father had aspirations to become a country landowner.
*Photograph: gelatin silver bromide print*
*196x131mm*
V&A (Linder Bequest)

▷ **Beatrix with Benjamin Bunny at Bolton Gardens**
***April 1890***
Beatrix, in a deerstalker, holds up Benjamin Bounce, 'a fascinating little beggar'. She had bought him in 1885 'from a London bird shop in a paper bag. His existence was not observed by the nursery authorities for a week.'

Benjamin modelled for her first published work, the greetings cards. Delighted with their success, she rewarded him with intoxicating hempseed.
*Photoprint (original 143x103mm)*
Cotsen

◁ **Beatrix at twenty-six, with rose**
***[1892]***
Studio portrait by A. F. Mackenzie of Birnam, Perthshire, who also photographed the painter Millais. Beatrix is fashionably dressed in gigot sleeves; she approved of the current style of dress.
*Photograph: albumen print (gold tinted)*
*150x88mm*
V&A (Linder Bequest)

▷ **Beatrix with Rupert and Bertram Potter at Heath Park, Birnam**
***12 October 1892***
The ever-recurring trio of Rupert, Beatrix and Bertram was a favourite subject, outnumbered only by portraits of Beatrix herself.

Of all her family, 'it was her brother first, then her father whom she cared for' (Caroline Hutton to William Heelis, 1944).
*Photograph: modern develop out print (silver gelatin paper)*
*229x195mm*
V&A (Linder Bequest)

△ **Beatrix with Border terrier at Lingholm, near Keswick**
***3 October 1897***
Hatless and smiling, Beatrix offers a titbit to the dog. Lingholm, where her family spent ten summers between 1885 and 1907, provided Derwentwater backgrounds for *The Tale of Squirrel Nutkin*.
*Photoprint (original 82x107mm)*
Cotsen

# NATURAL HISTORY AND ARTEFACTS

## Beatrix Potter the naturalist

Beatrix Potter belonged to 'the last generation that did not see the arts and science as mutually exclusive; rather science provided a firmer foundation for aesthetic response' (R. Fairley, on Jemima Blackburn). From earliest childhood Beatrix drew a whole menagerie of pets, kept upstairs in the schoolroom and taken on holiday in hutches: newts and lizards, snails ('they have such a surprising difference of character'), bats and mice – and rabbits. Already a serious naturalist at the age of nine, by eighteen she was scrutinizing spiders and insects in textbooks, showcases and under her brother's microscope; soon she was exploring the Zoological Gardens for exotic animals and the Natural History Museum for stuffed ones. Holiday escapes from London gave her the chance to extend her repertoire and study animals in the wild. By 1890 the 'funguses' had captured her imagination: they 'raised her spirits' and inspired some of her best work.

Characteristic of Potter's time was the passion for examining, cataloguing and explaining the natural world, as advocated by John Ruskin; following a centuries-old tradition, she inscribes her studies 'drawn from life'. She surpasses her contemporaries in the careful accuracy of her observation, and in her questioning, analytical approach. Drawings and discoveries remained unacknowledged, and so, in compensation, the books were born – but her science brought an extra dimension to the Tales.

# Fauna

◁ **Studies of Xarifa, a Hazel Dormouse**
**(*Muscardinus avellanarius*)**
***11 December 1887 [1886]***
Beatrix celebrates Xarifa, 'a sleepy little animal', in her Journal: 'I wonder if ever another dormouse had so many acquaintances, Mr. Bright, Mr. J. Millais, and Mr. Leigh Smith had admired and stroked her, amongst others. I think she was in many respects the sweetest little animal I ever knew.'
*Pen-and-ink over pencil*
*image 169x108mm on sheet 177x113mm*
V&A (Linder Bequest)

▷ **Beatrix with her pet dormouse Xarifa**
***1885***
Convalescent and with cropped hair, Beatrix holds Xarifa high for the camera. Many years later she endorsed this picture: 'Age 19 – much out of health Hair cut short!'

Xarifa and her unusual name, taken from one of the *Ancient Spanish Ballads* by J. G. Lockhart, were reborn forty years later as a character in *The Fairy Caravan*.
*Photoprint (original 163x155mm)*
Cotsen

▷ **Wood Mouse (*Apodemus sylvaticus*)**
***September 1886***
Inscribed 'Ring (or possibly "Long") tailed Field mouse' and painted at Camfield Place, Essex, almost identical to another mouse drawn as a Christmas gift in the same year. Potter's technique perfectly conveys the lithe form beneath the fur. Mice were fascinating subjects; she grew 'a little tired of rabbits'.
*Watercolour, bodycolour and pen-and-ink over pencil, with highlights in white paint image 57x76mm on sheet 76x114mm*
PC

▽ **Skull of a wolf**

***1 January 1886***

One of several skull subjects thought to have been taken from museum specimens, or from books.

This skull, and the studies of Xarifa, are examples of a short-lived experiment with Indian ink and a fine nib, used also for illustrations and interiors.

*Pen-and-ink over pencil, with a little white paint*
*image 69x142mm on sheet 120x224mm*
V&A (Linder Bequest)

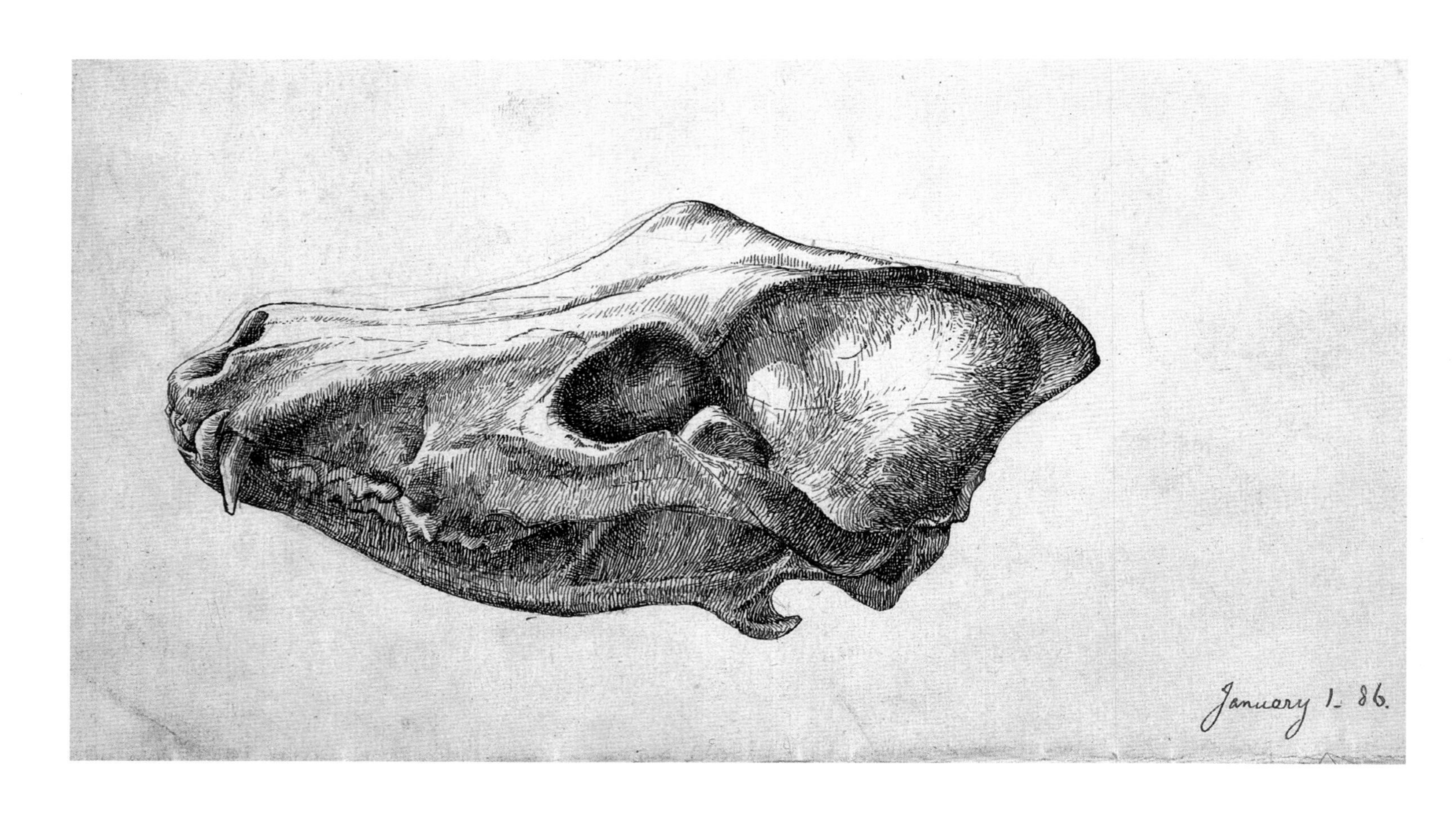

▷ **'Long-eared bats disputing with a common bat [Pipistrelle] for possession of the roosting place drawn from tame animals'**
***[ca. 1886]***
Between 1884 and 1888 Beatrix made at least twenty studies of bats, some rare – crouching, hanging, flying, or stripped to their skeletons. Remarkably, the bats' natural behaviour has been observed in a domestic interior.
*Watercolour*
*image 187x80mm on sheet 187x80mm*
AT

▽ **Dead stag, copied from a lithograph after Sir Edwin Landseer**
*[1884?]*
Among the sometimes unforgiving art criticisms in Beatrix Potter's Journal is one of Landseer and his 'sleek pretty creatures' (3 May 1888). Though impressed by much of Landseer's work, the eighteen-year-old Beatrix compares it unfavourably with that of Rosa Bonheur, who gives us the 'real view, long-boned wild animals'; Potter's stag, though dead, is considerably livelier than Landseer's.
*Black, red and white chalks over pencil, on grey paper*
*image as sheet 338x444mm (unevenly trimmed)*
V&A (Linder Bequest)

▷ **'Roedeer's Head drawn from a stuffed specimen, natural size'**
*[1895?]*
Probably drawn at the British Museum (Natural History), now the Natural History Museum. Beatrix found the exaggerated propriety of the Museum staff intimidating, and wrote: 'I never saw anything so fearful as the stuffed animals.'
*Watercolour (grey washes) over pencil image 292x188mm on sheet 369x290mm (unevenly trimmed); corners marked to give 330x229mm*
LT

'I never saw anything so fearful as the stuffed animals ... '

*Journal* 20 December 1895

◁ **Two squirrels on a log**
*[ca. 1895]*
Every detail has been carefully observed and recorded: the texture of the bark and the annual rings exposed at the cut end of the trunk.

This painting, paired with a back view, was intended for a greetings card but never published. Potter planned several 'shaped' cards, but Hildesheimer & Faulkner printed only a pair of designs showing mice inside a coconut. In 1926 Frederick Warne considered these squirrels as possible covers for a calendar; she suggested that they might also be used inside, to illustrate 'October'.
*Watercolour over pencil, with some highlights in white paint, on thin card*
*image 127x102mm on sheet 210x182mm*
V&A (Linder Bequest)

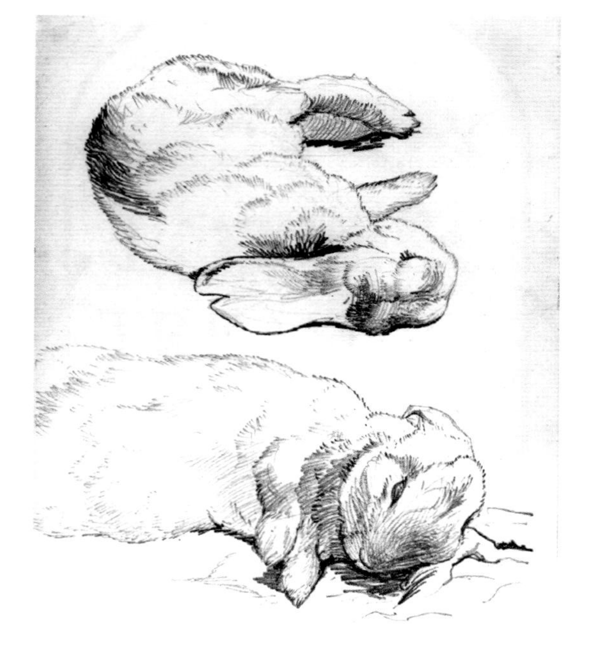

◁ **Peter Rabbit**
*[1899?]*
The original Peter, 'an affectionate companion and a quiet friend'. Acquired in 1892, he died on 26th January 1901, not long before the *Peter Rabbit* drawings were begun.
*Pencil*
*image 196x168mm on sheet 250x176mm*
LT

▷ **'A Dream of Toasted Cheese'**
***1899***

Beatrix presented this picture to her impressive uncle Sir Henry Roscoe, F.R.S., in honour of his textbook, *First Step in Chemistry*. Finding it 'as original as it is humorous', he reproduced it in his memoirs, enjoying her sly topical references to $NH_3$ (ammonia gas) and the Bunsen burner, a recent invention of his former mentor at Heidelberg.

The learned mouse, also drawn reading a newspaper, prefigures the mouse who sits upon a cotton reel on the cover of *The Tailor of Gloucester*.

*Watercolour and pen-and-ink*
*image 230x140mm on sheet 270x200mm*
PC

◁ **Squirrel**
***[1903]***
Volatile and hyperactive, squirrels were difficult models. Potter captures the essential quality of this individual, using an interesting combination of colours.

The sheet was detached from a sketchbook containing squirrel studies for *The Tale of Squirrel Nutkin* (1903) and cat studies for *The Tale of Benjamin Bunny* (1904).
*Watercolour over pencil, on rough-textured buff-tinted paper*
*image 111x115mm on sheet 174x217mm*
V&A (Linder Bequest)

▷ **Sketches of a sleeping cat, 'from life'**
***2 June 1903***
The female cat who lay so long on the basket in *The Tale of Benjamin Bunny* was modelled on Sarto, a surprisingly large-tailed tom. To satisfy her publisher, Potter later redrew him with a shorter tail. Her cat studies are more successful than her dogs, although she found cats difficult to draw.
*Watercolour over pencil; pencil*
*images 214x250mm on sheet 229x292mm*
V&A (Linder Bequest)

'I see no reason why common-sense should not foster a healthier appreciation of beauty than morbid sentimentality.'

*Journal* 5 June 1891

▷ **Cat on swill-basket, from *The Tale of Benjamin Bunny* (page 45)**
***1904***
The cat came and sniffed at the basket, then she 'sat there for *five hours*'. The model was a male cat. 'I think that Sarto quite gives a tone to the book – he is so handsome and aristocratic,' Beatrix wrote to his owner, Sir James Vaughan; and she added him to an endpaper.

▽ **Studies of a dead thrush**

***1902***

'Picked up dead in the snow' at Woodcote in Surrey, home of Beatrix Potter's uncle, the distinguished scientist and educator Sir Henry Roscoe. The bird, seen from several angles, is recorded with a naturalist's eye and a clear, transparent palette.

*Watercolour and pen-and-ink over pencil*
*image 217x269mm on sheet 229x293mm*
V&A (Linder Bequest)

△ **'Hen Blackbird drawn from nature'**
*[ca. 1905?]*
Some of Beatrix Potter's earliest extant drawings are studies of dead creatures; this example is reminiscent of a bird study by Jemima Blackburn. Familiar with the work of Bewick, Weir and Gould, Beatrix also much admired Thorburn's paintings of birds in landscapes. Here, however, she considers her subject as a specimen.
*Watercolour over pencil, with highlights in white paint*
*image 140x220mm on sheet 210x295mm*
FLP

◁ **Magpie, from a sketchbook**
***[1905]***
These studies, made at the Zoological Gardens, are annotated with details of shape and colour: 'brown black eye nose a little hookyer [*sic*] than jackdaw, less feathered'. Potter's observations of animals, often recorded in her Journal, could be called on later for her books.
*Pencil*
*128x182mm (opening), 139x97mm (book)*
V&A (Linder Bequest)

▽ **'Dr. Maggotty's Mixture',**
**from *The Pie and the Patty-Pan* (page 45)**
***1905***
Figures and scenes in Beatrix Potter's sketchbooks metamorphosed into 'book pictures'. Dr. Maggotty was modelled on the magpies at the Zoological Gardens (now the London Zoo at Regent's Park).

▷ **Blue tit**
*[ca. 1910?]*
One of Potter's lively and spontaneous working drawings: she covered sheet after sheet with swift impressions – of several animals, of one animal, or of a single arresting feature. One such sheet is humorously inscribed 'Studies of a Teddy Bear!'
*Watercolour with some pencil*
*image 242x155mm on sheet 253x177mm*
FLP

◁ **Small and Large White Butterflies (*Pieris rapae* and *Pieris brassicae*, females), with magnified wing scales**
***[1887?]***
Attached to the verso are Potter's record notes: 'Cabbage butterflies – AA parts of wings seen through microscope showing the scales, (which rub off like dust on the fingers when one touches a moth or butterfly)'.
*Watercolour and pen-and-ink, with highlights in white paint, wing details in pencil frame*
*image 263x220mm on sheet 364x269mm*
FLP

▷ ***Diaptomus castor*: a freshwater planktonic copepod**
***1 April 1887***
Beatrix Potter's microscope work was both appealing and accurate. She drew at various magnifications, sometimes using mounted specimens from her brother's entomological cabinet. This study, made at Camfield, shows dorsal and lateral views of an adult male.
*Watercolour and pen-and-ink over pencil*
*image 317x228mm on sheet 367x269mm*
LT

▷ **Male Jumping Spider (*Salticus sp. scenicus*), magnified**
***May 1886***
One of at least a dozen microscope paintings of spiders; most were done in 1887, but three almost identical studies of this Jumping Spider date from 1886. Sketches of spiders and ladybirds for *The Tale of Mrs. Tittlemouse* are looser and more impressionistic.
*Watercolour, with highlights in white paint*
*image 290x255mm on sheet 365x269mm*
FLP

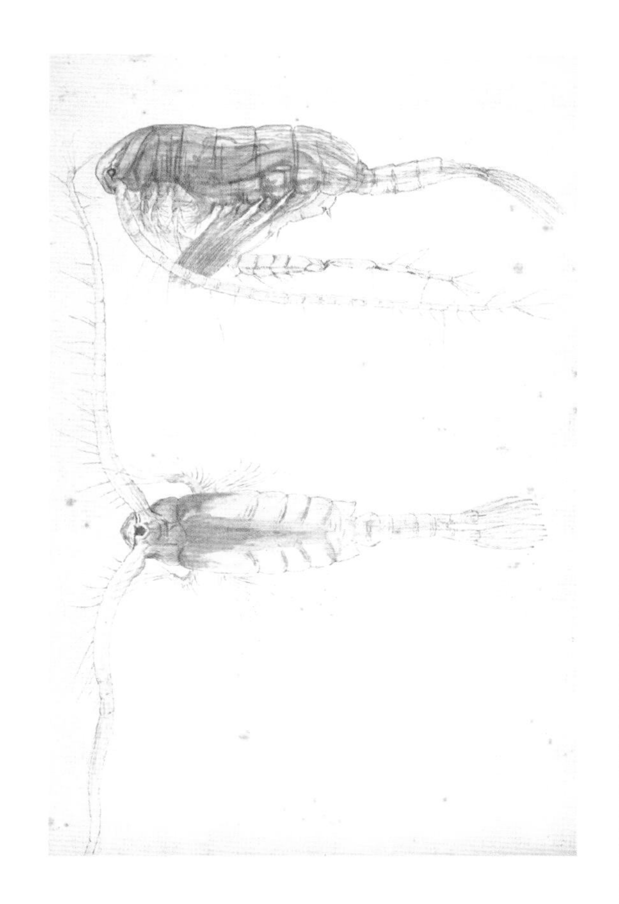

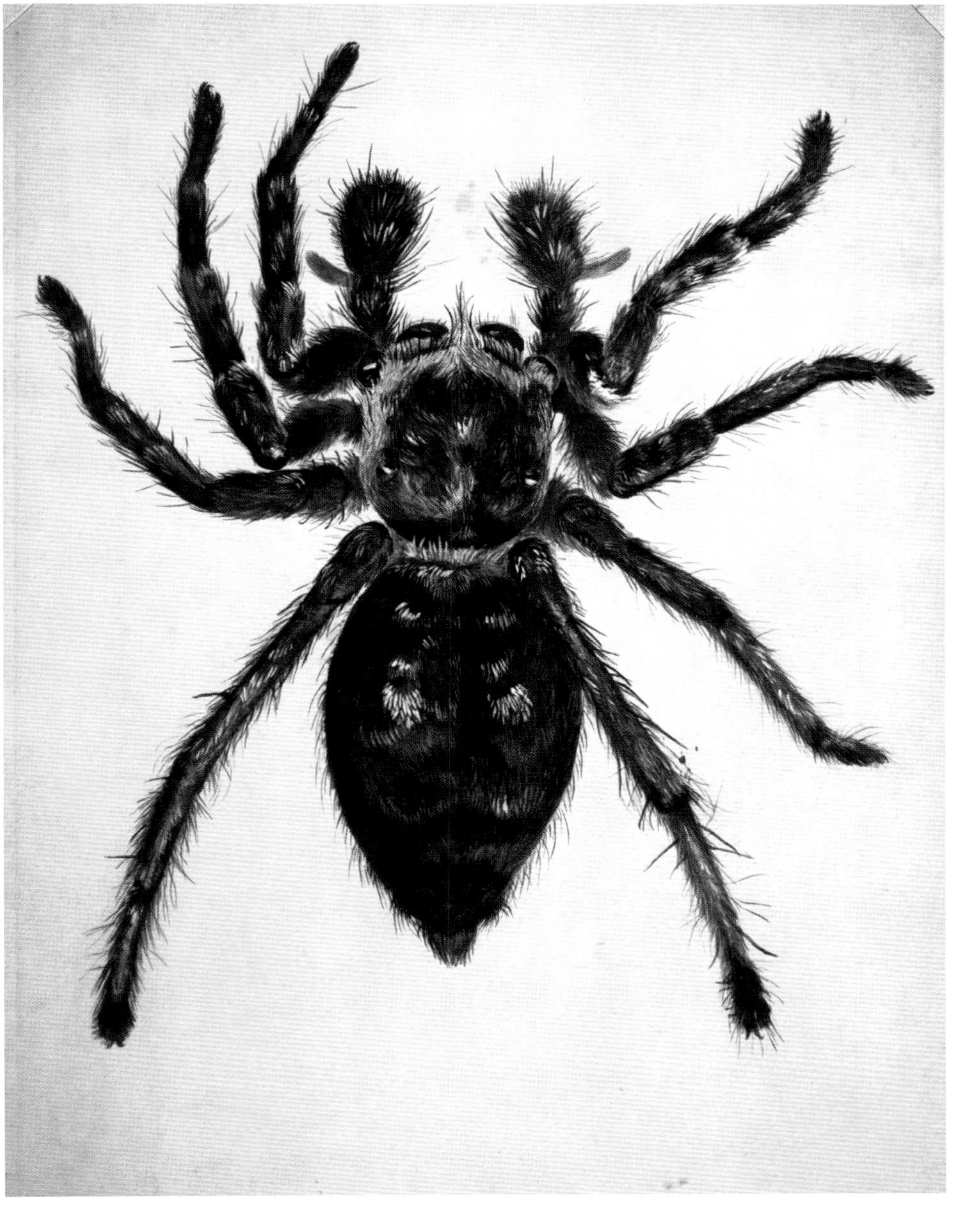

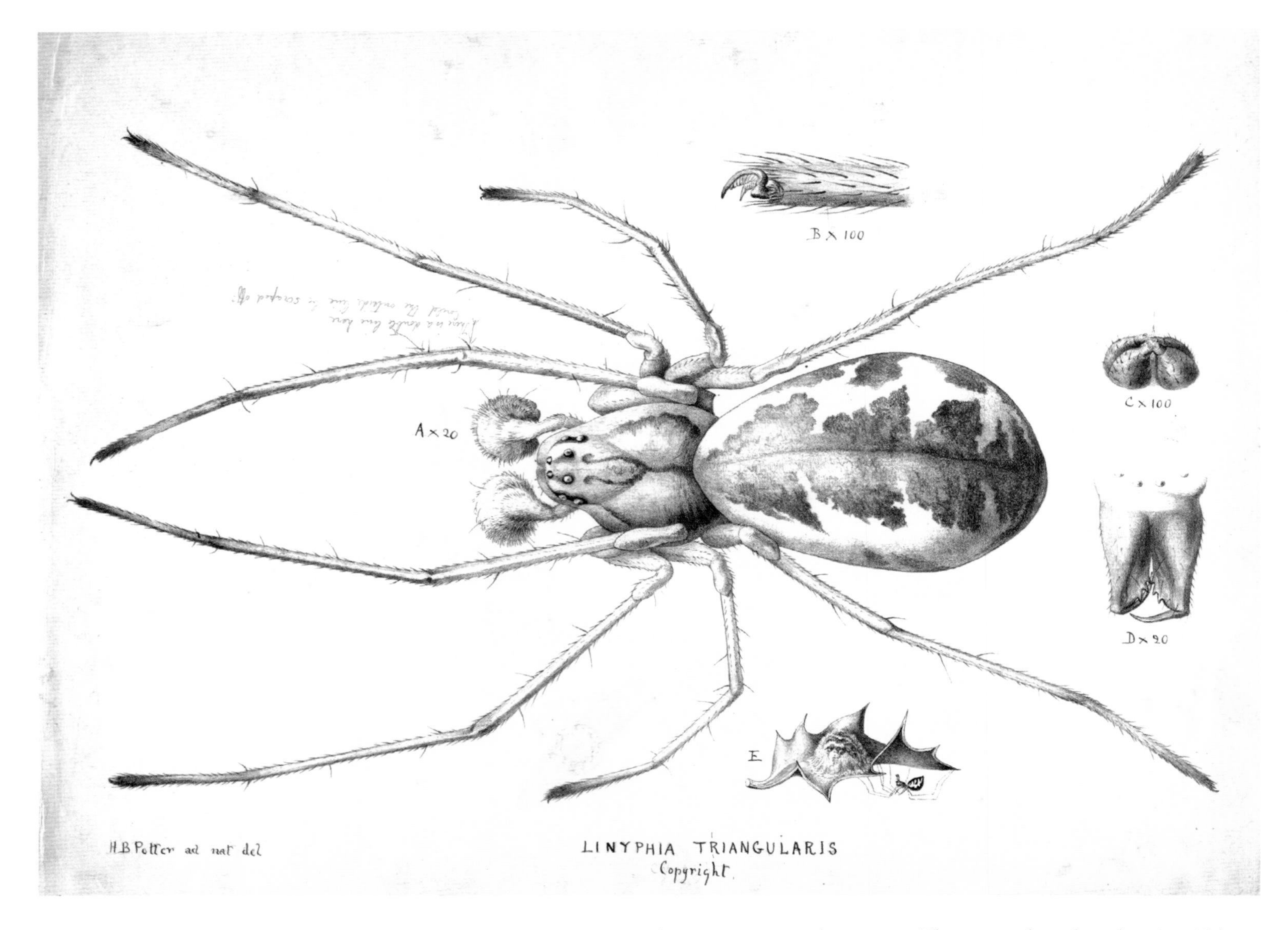


△ **Sheet Web Spider (*Linyphia triangularis*)** ***[1896]***
One of only two known lithographed plates from a projected set of twelve, apparently commissioned for the British Museum (Natural History) by Miss Caroline Martineau in 1895–96, and inscribed with Potter's instructions to the lithographer. The series would have brought together her entomological work, done ten years earlier; apart from this spider only the Privet Hawk Moth survives, and a 'trial run' of miscellaneous items including fungi.

The set was planned as a learning aid, but Potter doubted whether the plates were of any educational value 'because they were not drawn with design'. Her approach was nonetheless thoroughly professional. The spider is examined at different magnifications, with details drawn at x 100 and x 20; holly leaf and spider (E) are actual size.
*Lithograph and pen-and-ink over erased pencil, on thin card*
*images (including inscriptions) 240x352mm on sheet 280x378mm*
V&A (Linder Bequest)

▽ **'Boar fish full size', with sea anemone**
***14 April 1895***
'In the morning I picked up a strange little red fish which I painted,' Beatrix records at Weymouth, where the family was spending its customary bracing spring holiday by the sea. This arresting portrait is comparable in quality with her best fungus and fossil studies.
*Watercolour over pencil, with highlights in white paint; pen-and-ink (sea anemone)*
*images 118x161mm on sheet 199x261mm*
V&A (Linder Bequest)

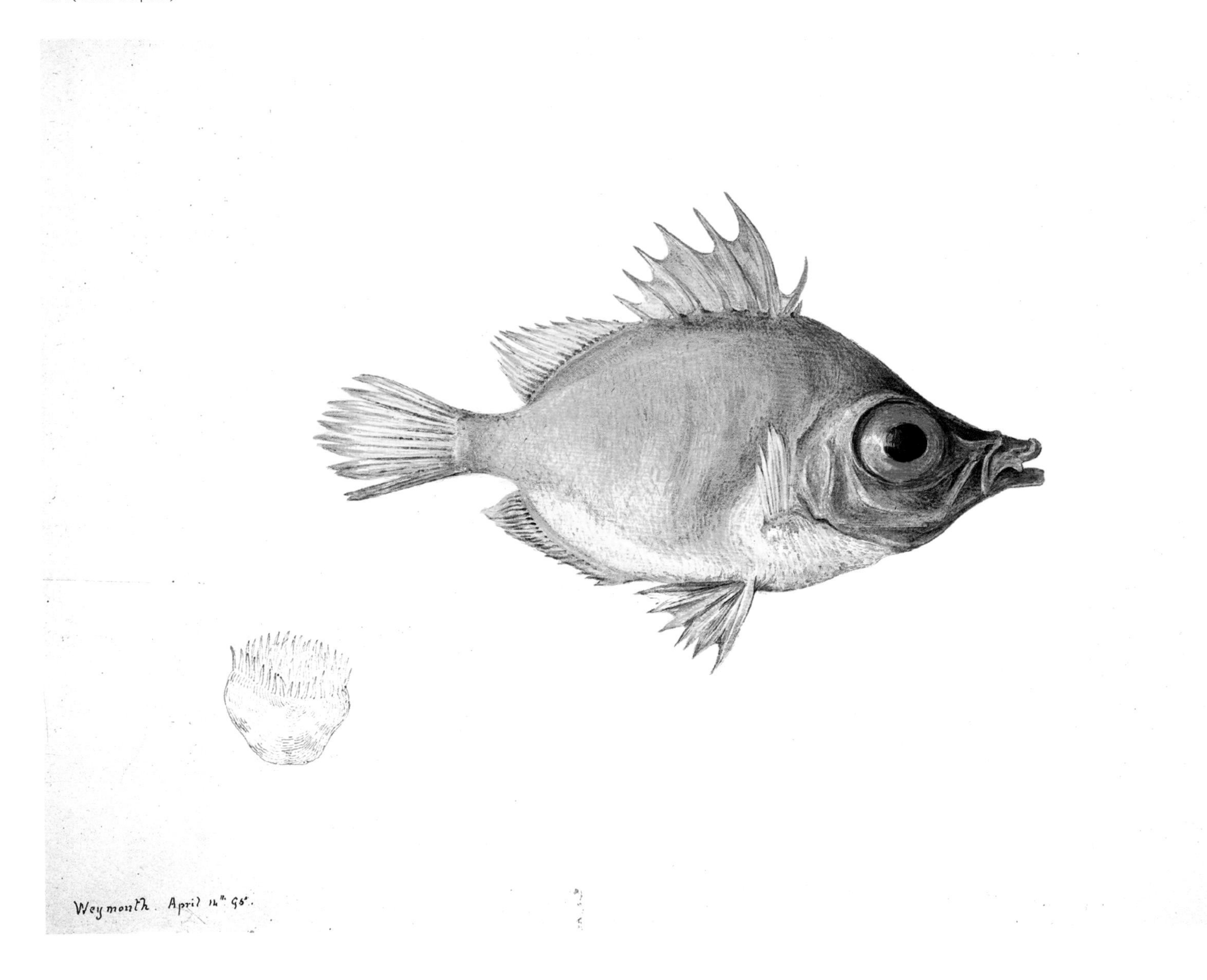

# ‘All writers for children ought to have a sufficient recognition of what things look like ... ’

**26 June 1942, to Mrs. Wight**

◁ **Frogs**
*[ca. 1905?]*
A characteristic collection of animal attitudes. Potter drew newts and lizards, frogs and toads, and understood their behaviour. She criticized Kenneth Grahame for flying in the face of nature by making Mr. Toad comb his hair: ‘all writers for children ought to have a sufficient recognition of what things look like.’
*Pencil*
*image 185x165mm on sheet 205x168mm*
V&A (Linder Bequest)

▷ **'A great big enormous trout seized Mr. Jeremy with a snap', from *The Tale of Mr. Jeremy Fisher* (page 41)**
***1906***

Three of Potter's tales significantly reflect her knowledge of flora, fauna and habitat: *Squirrel Nutkin, Mrs. Tittlemouse* and *Mr. Jeremy Fisher*.

Fish, with their variety of lustre and colour, are ideal subjects for the artist, according to William Henry Hunt, that Victorian painter of exquisite detail.

*Watercolour and pen-and-ink over erased pencil image (vignetted) 106x93mm on sheet 127x108mm*

NT

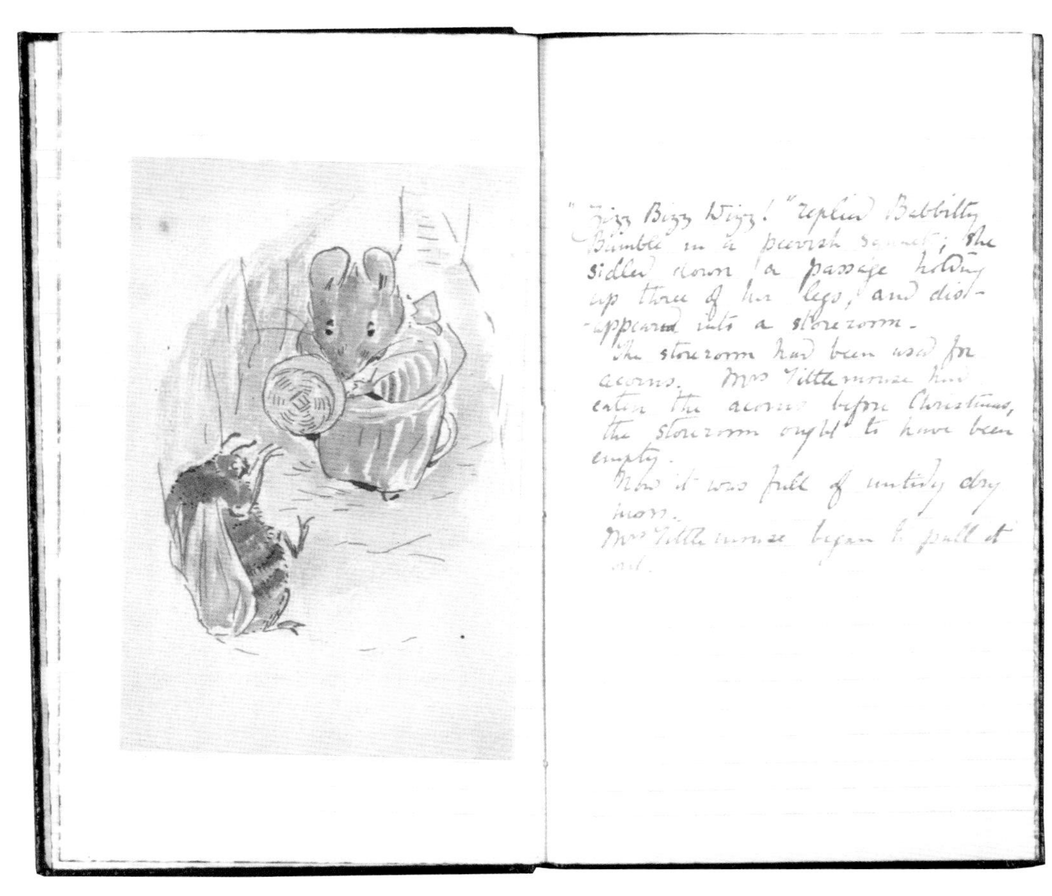

"Bizz Bizz Wizz!" replied Babbitty Bumble in a peevish squeak; she sidled down a passage holding up three of her legs, and dis-appeared into a storeroom.
The storeroom had been used for acorns. Mrs Tittlemouse had eaten the acorns before Christmas, the storeroom ought to have been empty.
Now it was full of untidy dry moss.
Mrs Tittlemouse began to pull at

▷ **Wood mouse and bumble bee, from the 1910 presentation manuscript of 'The Tale of Mrs. Tittlemouse' (facsimile by Decimus Publishing)**
***1979***

Insects and spiders scuttle through the corridors, and each creature behaves according to its nature. The fastidious heroine is plagued by unwanted 'friends' (altered by Frederick Warne to 'visitors'). Beatrix was forced to make other changes: a ground beetle replaces the earwig, woodlice are mere 'creepy-crawly people', and the centipede is cut out altogether.

Given to Nellie Warne for New Year 1910, the original morocco-bound booklet had only eight watercolours, expanded to twenty-eight coloured illustrations for the Warne edition.

*Watercolour and sepia ink or paint (original MS) 90x64mm on sheet 112x73mm (original image, vignetted)*

PC

# Flora

◁ Posy of wild flowers
*[ca. 1885?]*
Except in her garden backgrounds, or in the complex substrates of fungus paintings, Potter usually examined individual plants, but this posy contains buttercup, clover, cornflower, cow parsley, dodder, forget-me-not, honeysuckle, knapweed, meadowsweet and orchis. Light and colour are more important than line.
*Watercolour over pencil*
*image 278x230mm on sheet 316x234mm*
LT

# 'It sometimes happens that the town child is more alive to the fresh beauty of the country than a child who is country born.'

'Roots' of the Peter Rabbit Tales, *Horn Book Magazine* May 1929

▷ Pine-cone (*Pinus sylvestris*)
*30 June 1895*
A powerfully three-dimensional plant portrait, viewed at eye-level.

Perhaps the subject reminded Potter of 'a rare fungus shaped like a pine-cone' (Old Man of the Woods, *Strobilomyces floccopus*), which she had discovered and painted at Eastwood on the River Tay nearly two years earlier. The next day, she drew her first version of the Peter Rabbit story and sent it to a young friend.
*Watercolour over pencil*
*image 95x140mm on sheet 200x260mm*
LT

▽ **Spray of Sweet Bay (*Magnolia virginiana*)**
***February 1900***
Beatrix Potter has annotated this drawing as both naturalist and practical artist: 'against the light', and 'the veins in the leaf are slightly transparent – There has been no sunshine, & evergreen leaves show very little transparent light without it.' Arrows indicate the direction of the light.
*Watercolour and pen-and-ink over pencil image (including inscriptions) 169x242mm on sheet 178x254mm*
V&A (Linder Bequest)

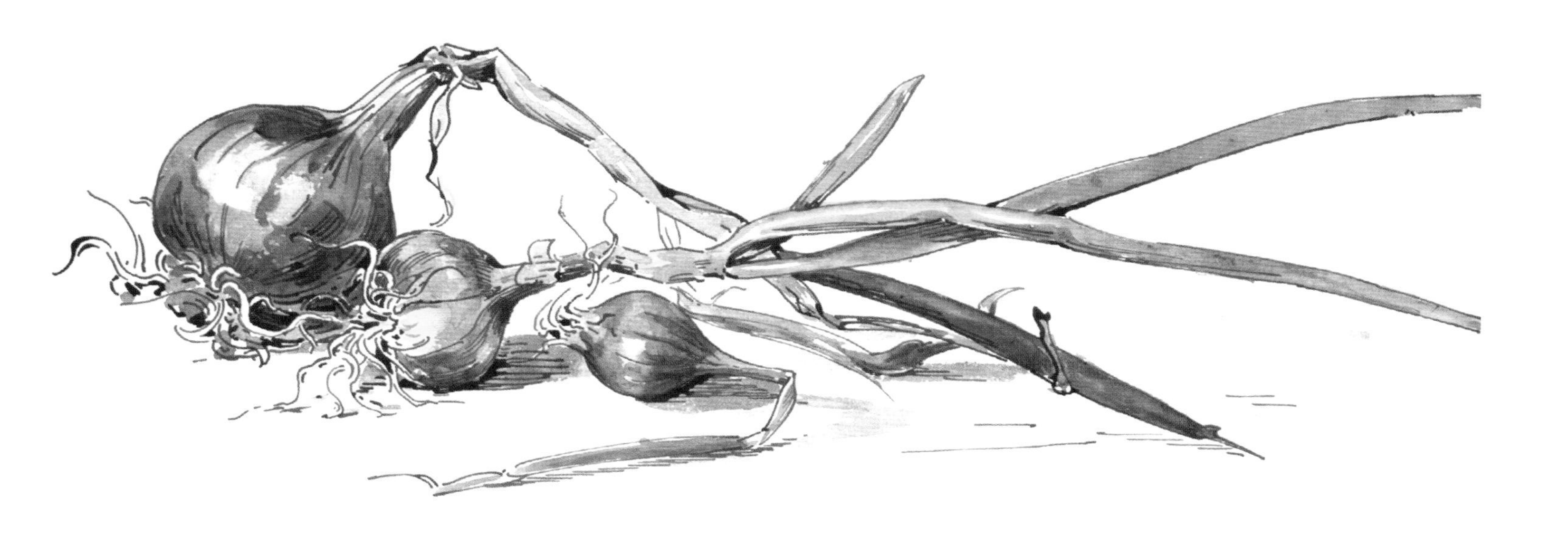

△ **Onions at Fawe Park, Derwentwater**
***26 August 1903***
One of several groups of onions drawn while collecting garden backgrounds for *The Tale of Benjamin Bunny* (1904), both for their interesting visual qualities, and to get the detail right. The fluent sepia line, made glossy by added gum arabic, is enhanced with translucent wash.
*Watercolour and sepia ink or paint over pencil*
*image 96x289mm on sheet 213x292mm*
V&A (Linder Bequest)

# Fungi

◁ ***Hygrophorus sub-radiatus*** **from Holehird, Windermere**
***17 September 1895***
Living fungi drawn in their natural habitat were preferable to dried specimens sent during the winter months. The grassy substrate of this fungus reappears in *The Tale of Mr. Jeremy Fisher* (*see page 115*).

As with her book illustrations, Potter's usual method was to draw the background first, and then put in the figure – face or fungus. Larger specimens dominate, while diagrammatic elements lie discreetly behind or (as here) at one side.
*Watercolour over pencil*
*image 160x230mm on sheet 210x275mm*
AT

**'Now of all hopeless things to draw ... the very worst is a fine fat fungus,'** Potter wrote ruefully in 1892. Historically, fungus illustration had been slow to develop, partly because the anatomy of fungi was poorly understood. Captivated by their striking shapes and colours, she began to draw fungi in the late 1880s. Even her earliest attempts, though scientifically amateurish, were both accurate and aesthetically attractive. Advice from Charles McIntosh, the Perthshire naturalist, taught her a more systematic approach, and her drawings became scientific documents (R. Watling). Encouragement came from her eminent uncle, Sir Henry Roscoe, who provided up-to-date equipment, and helped her to understand Pasteur and Brefeld on the culture of micro-organisms. Fungi and spores, mosses and lichens inspired over five hundred studies, all drawn without aids such as a camera lucida.

The first person in Britain to succeed in making time lapse drawings of the germination of spores of agarics, and in non-sterile conditions, Potter was also one of the first to realize the symbiotic, dual nature of lichens, recording also the mutual association of different fungi. In 1897 she submitted a paper (now lost) on the germination of the spores of agarics to the Linnean Society. As an amateur and a woman, she shocked the academic establishment by making independent experiments and developing theories. Potter's work as a mycologist can now at last be appreciated by a wider audience. Her drawings identify many distinct species only recently recognized – and modern mycologists realize how close she came to discovering *Penicillium*.

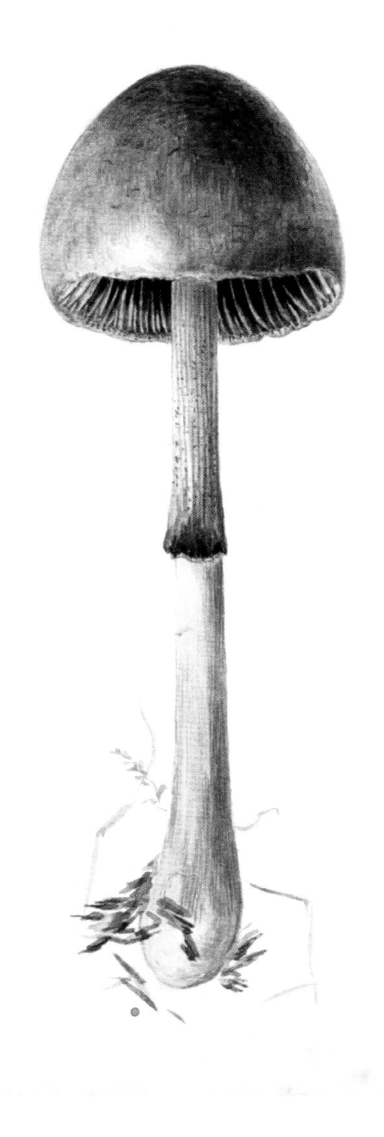

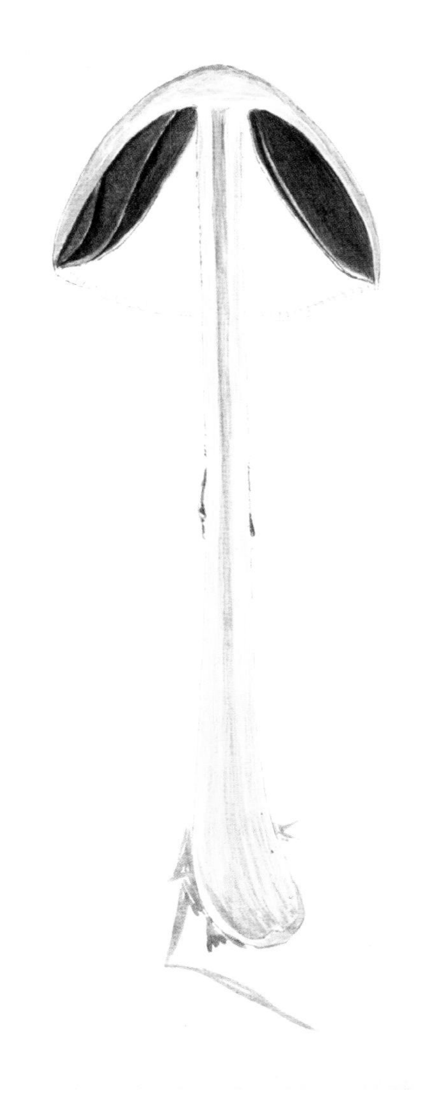

△ **Dung Mottle Gill (*Panaeolus semiovatus*, formerly *campanulatus*) from Smailholm Tower near Kelso**
***25 September 1894***
Potter's fungus studies show a degree of knowledge and attention to detail unusual for the time. By now, she had the skill to draw specimens without setting. This long section (*right*) shows cap, stem and gills, according to the instructions on botanical drawing she had received from Charlie McIntosh, postman and naturalist, and a strong contendant for her composite portrait of Mr. McGregor.
*Watercolour over pencil*
*image 170x160mm on sheet 215x280mm*
AT

'Now of all hopeless things to draw ... the very worst is a fine fat fungus.'

*Journal* 29 October 1892

▽ **Slimy Spike Cap (*Gomphidius glutinosus*)**
**from Hatchednize Wood, Coldstream**
***18 August 1894***
In the Scottish Borders Beatrix was 'overtaken with funguses'. 'I found … joy of joys, the spiky *Gomphidius glutinosus*, a round, slimy, purple head among the moss. … There is extreme complacency in finding a totally new species for the first time.' (*Journal*, 18 August 1894)

Protected from the light in specially made fabric portfolios, her fungus paintings have kept their fresh colours.
*Watercolour over pencil, with highlights in white paint*
*image 170x200mm on sheet 215x280mm*
AT

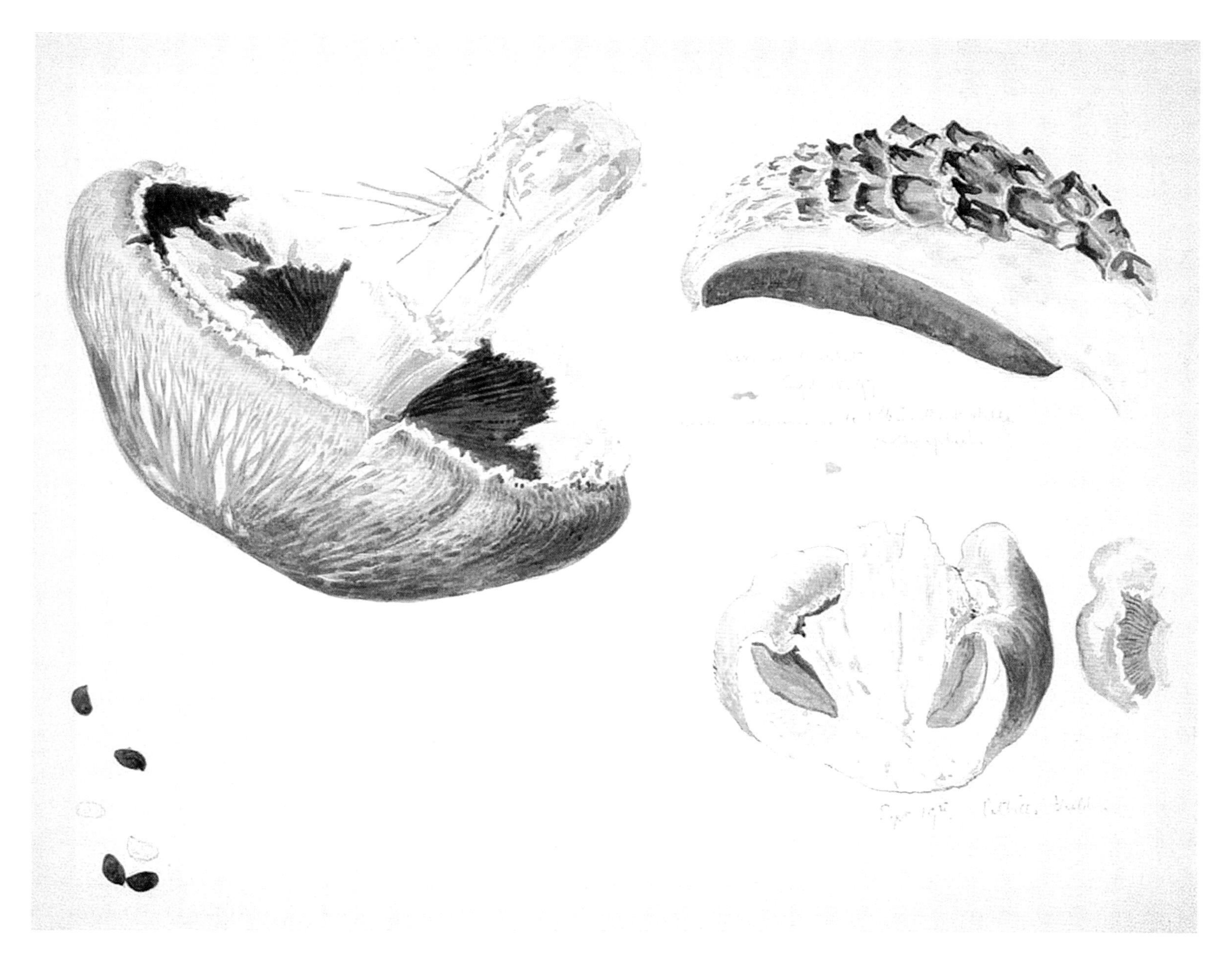

△ **Common Field Mushroom (*Agaricus campestris* var. *hortensis*)**
***15 September 1897***
The edible commercial mushroom: one from Keswick Market, and others photographed a few days later at 'Catbells Field', as indicated in the inscriptions. Specimens were often drawn upside-down, so as to show the under-surface, and studied from all angles as a sculptor surveys a human head.
*Watercolour over pencil*
*image 220x245mm on sheet 240x300mm*
AT

△ **Market scenes from the 'Derwentwater Sketchbook',** ***1903***
**(facsimile published by Frederick Warne** ***1984*****)**
Drawn at the Saturday Market in Keswick on 19 September 1903: fruit and vegetable stalls – and people. Potter did not make a serious study of human anatomy, but her attempts at figure drawing were much more successful when she did not try too hard, as in her picture letters and sketchbooks.
*91x267mm (each opening)*
WA

▷ **Little Red Riding Hood encounters the Wolf** *[1894]*

Ferns in the high wall and Mycena-like fungi in the foreground contribute to a sensation of claustrophobia and damp. Beatrix Potter occasionally used human models, including 'Parton's little boy' at Harescombe Grange for the seated Tailor of Gloucester. Beatrix Potter photographed his sister in August 1894 as an aid to drawing a companion front view to illustrate this fairy tale from Perrault (*see also pages 90–91*).

*Watercolour (grey washes), bodycolour and pen-and-ink, with highlights in white paint, pencil frame*

*image ca. 188x131mm on sheet 261x178mm*

FLP

◁ **Preliminary studies for 'The Toads' Tea Party'**

***[1902?]***

One toad drinks tea with little finger cocked; a less genteel guest is eating a large slice of cake. Roughed out table and chairs are gill fungi, and there are two toads fewer than in the finished painting.

*Pencil*

*upper image 100x126mm, lower image 64x128mm, on sheet 209x153mm (unevenly trimmed)*

LT

◁ **'The Toads' Tea Party'**

***[1902?]***

Toads and toadstools: the gill fungi have become bun-shaped Boletes. Exquisite petal and leaf tints contrast with squat shapes which conform with the rounded vignette. A decorative border of acorns and twigs was originally envisaged for this design. It illustrates the rhyme 'If acorn cups were tea-cups', but the tea is laced with honey-dew, exudate of the ergot fungus.

*Watercolour and sepia ink or paint over erased pencil, with highlights in white paint*

*image (vignetted) 118x116mm on sheet 202x162mm*

V&A (Linder Bequest)

△ **Agarics, from *The Tale of Squirrel Nutkin* (page 26)**
***1903***
Some of Potter's earliest and latest fungus paintings were done when staying at Lingholm on Derwentwater, where she drew the backgrounds for *Squirrel Nutkin*. This is the only published Tale to include mushrooms in its autumnal setting: aptly, since squirrels eat them.

▷ **'I should not choose to spend a night in Pringle Wood myself', from *The Fairy Caravan* (page 90)**
***1929***
Only rarely does Potter use fungi decoratively or whimsically, or in the backgrounds of her books. In *The Fairy Caravan* she displays her knowledge of herbalism, and fungi play an active part in the plot. Paddy Pig, suffering from the after-effects of 'toadstool tartlets', huddles inside a hollow tree, roped in by cobwebs. Oppressed by bracket fungi and agarics, spider and toad, elves, and nameless 'things', he is cured at last by an infusion of rue, the Herb of Grace.

# Fossils

◁ **Eight fossils from the Applethwaite Beds, Troutbeck, near Windermere**
***15 November 1895***
Beatrix collected these fossils in August and September, and drew them later in London. After 1901 both fungi and fossils occupied her less often, but in 1904 she returned to the fossils for recreation.

The complicated textures of rocks and fossils fascinated nineteenth-century artists. Beatrix Potter photographed her finds, and she painted them in a hard-edged, quasi-photographic technique suited to their lichened greys and browns – superior to any photograph in rendering solidity and texture.
*Watercolour over pencil*
*images 208x175mm on sheet 245x195mm*
NT

▷ **Roman needles and toilet utensils from Bucklersbury**
***22 October 1894***
Excavations in Queen Victoria Street, City of London, in 1872-73 brought to light a number of Roman and post-Roman objects, found in the silts of the ancient Walbrook stream. The artefacts were lent to Beatrix Potter twenty-one years later by their owner, Mr. Tom H. Squire; most have since disappeared, and her carefully scaled drawings are the only surviving records.
*Watercolour over pencil*
*image 255x175mm on sheet 260x200mm*
AT

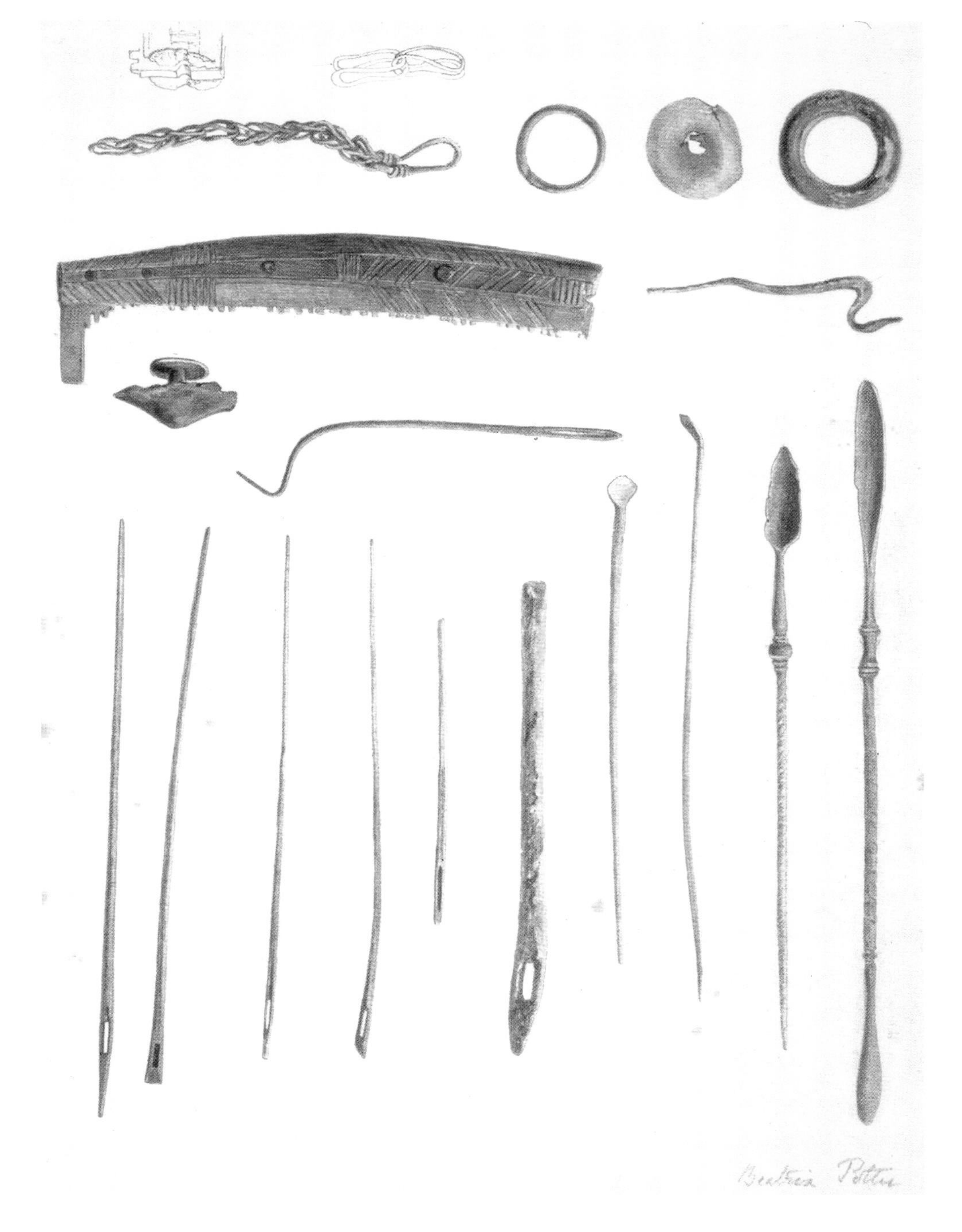

◁ **Sole of a mediaeval shoe**
***March 1895***
Beatrix Potter knew how to isolate an object and analyse its intrinsic qualities. Her drawings reflect the contemporary conventional approach to archaeological artefacts, but they are no mere inventories.

She had the amateur's freedom from professional inhibition, and could explore shape and colour, and the knobby hardness of a shoe leather with its imprint of the original owner.
*Watercolour over pencil*
*image 255x260mm on sheet 380x325mm*
AT

'Last time … I caught myself in the back yard making a careful and admiring copy of the swill bucket, and the laugh it gave me brought me round.'

*Journal* 4 October 1884

# THE YOUNG ARTIST

# Family background and early work

## Early life and influences

'Thank goodness, my education was neglected; I was never sent to school . . . it would have rubbed off some of the originality,' Beatrix Potter wrote in 1929. On the contrary, much care was taken over her education, and her talents were encouraged at home. She absorbed much, too, from a cultivated Radical milieu. Exposed to pictures and conversations, and to *Punch*, she relished the caricatures of Phiz and Cruikshank, Leech and Doyle. All the Potters drew and copied; and Rupert Potter collected the works of Caldecott; both her parents and her brother Bertram shared her love of animals and art.

Beatrix had few children's books, but soon encountered great literature: Dickens, Jane Austen and Shakespeare, John Bunyan and the Bible. Imaginative reading was encouraged: Lear at four-and-a-half and *Alice* at the age of six or seven. From her Highland nurse she absorbed folklore and fairy tale; from a lucky succession of well-chosen governesses, sympathetic to her interests, she learnt French and Latin, and then German. Between the ages of twelve and seventeen she studied 'freehand, model drawing, geometry, perspective and a little water-colour flower painting' from Miss Cameron, who fifteen years later sent her fungi to draw from France. In 1880 and 1881 she took her only formal qualification, the Art Student's Certificate (2nd Grade) at the National Art Training School in South Kensington, conveniently near home.

Gallery visiting gave her the opportunity to study both the Old Masters and the fashions of the day. Encouraged by their example, she wistfully admired the work of women artists: Angelica Kauffmann, Louisa Waterford, Jemima Blackburn and Rosa Bonheur – even Kate Greenaway (though she 'can't draw'). In 1883 there had been a brief and distressing flirtation with oil painting, which she disliked: 'I can't bear those horrid paints, and they've put me out for using my own'. Fearing 'infection' from the wrong training, or from another artist's style, she exclaimed, 'It is a risky thing to copy, shall I catch it?' She disapproved of artistic theft, and was sensitive to accusations of plagiarism, but freely admitted the influence on her work of Randolph Caldecott: 'I have the greatest admiration for his work – a jealous appreciation; for I think that others, whose names are commonly bracketted with his, are not on the same plane at all as artist-illustrators.' Turner impressed her most of all, as 'the greatest landscape painter that ever has lived'.

# 'It is all the same, drawing, painting, modelling, the irresistible desire to copy any beautiful object which strikes the eye. Why cannot one be content to look at it? I cannot rest, I must draw.'

***Journal* 4 October 1884**

## The young artist

Among the earliest surviving examples of Beatrix Potter's work are three home-made drawing books dating from Autumn 1875 and Spring 1876. The first and most fragile contains drawings of caterpillars accompanied by observation notes on their habits, evidence of a precociously methodical approach. She copied birds, humming birds and flowers as well as fantasy pictures, from natural history books, Jemima Blackburn and Walter Crane; but she also drew real buildings and landscapes. Already present is a sense of colour and composition, and a lively humour.

In 1876–1877, she was copying outlines from Vere Foster's series of drawing manuals – trees and flowers, animals, artefacts and buildings – and still signing her drawings 'Helen Beatrix Potter'; only the earliest works bear her full name. A decorative monogram was briefly used during the pen-and-ink phase of 1883–1887. Then, by the late 1880s, the initials 'HBP' start to appear, but only rarely after 1895. Source-material for transfer prints came from Vere Foster and from Blackburn's *Birds*; she moved on to Flaxman's *Classical Outlines*, illustrations to historical and literary texts, in particular the works of Sir Walter Scott, and to ballads, rhymes and fairy tales.

Experimenting with technique as well as style, Beatrix and her brother Bertram tried everything from lino cuts and etching to clay modelling, plaster plaques to Platinotype printing, painting on tiles and photography. By 1884, at the age of eighteen, she had become an accomplished and versatile artist.

▷ **Hares at play**
***1879***
This early humorous drawing was recently discovered among a collection of greetings cards sent to Bertram, then aged six. It has obvious similarities to another drawing done three years earlier (*see right*). On the back is one of Bertram's own scribbles, of animals in a landscape.

In these clothed animals Beatrix caricatures human activities. The hares (or a long-eared variety of rabbit) ride in a carriage and fish under a bridge; one seems to be training a dog! The setting is likely to be Perthshire, as hinted in the mountainous backdrop and boulder-strewn river: perhaps the River Tay, Mr. Jeremy Fisher's original habitat. Effectively placed in the composition is a pollarded willow, one of the subjects of her schoolroom art lessons.
*Pen-and-ink*
*image as sheet 77x113mm*
NT

▷ **Rabbits (or hares) skating, from a juvenile drawing book**
***March 1876***
Remarkable for their characterization and sense of movement are these early clothed-animal fantasies, drawn by Beatrix at the age of nine in pencil and pen-and-ink. Humorous drawings date back to her early childhood, though this aspect of her art was not to develop for another twenty years.
*Photoprint from a drawing book in the V&A*
V&A (Linder Bequest)

HBP 1576

◁ **Paintbox by Newman, Soho Square**
***[1878–1880]***

Fragments of Chinese ink were discovered in one compartment. In a 'secret' drawer were notes on flower paintings, a group of transfer prints from *The Pipits* (*see page* 65), and a drawing in violet ink.

The twelve colours provided were: Prussian Blue, Vermilion, Gamboge, Crimson Lake, Indigo, Vandyke Brown, Neutral Tint, Brown Pink, Light Red, Yellow Ochre, Emerald Green and Burnt Sienna. In *Peter Rabbit's Painting Book* (1911) Beatrix Potter advises the young artist: 'You will want a brush and 5 paints – Antwerp Blue, Crimson Lake, Gamboge, Sap Green and Burnt Sienna.' Apart from a few tantalising remarks in letters, complaining about lead white in general, and certain colourists in particular, Potter was reticent about the pigments she used, but for her own book pictures she favoured sap green, light red and mauve.

*Polished wood with brass lock*
*226x188x78mm high*
PC

▷ **Notes on colours, from the paintbox drawer**
***May–June 1880***

These records, made a few weeks before Beatrix Potter's fourteenth birthday, lay hidden for years. She refers to colours used in six flower paintings, with a general note on shading yellow flowers: Wallflowers (21–22 May), Geraniums (28 May), Yellow daisies (29 May), Rose leaves (3–4 June), Yellow flowers (3 June), Cornflowers (10 June), Cow daisies (10 June).

*Pencil, with ruled lines*
*2ff 4 pages, each 180x113mm*
PC

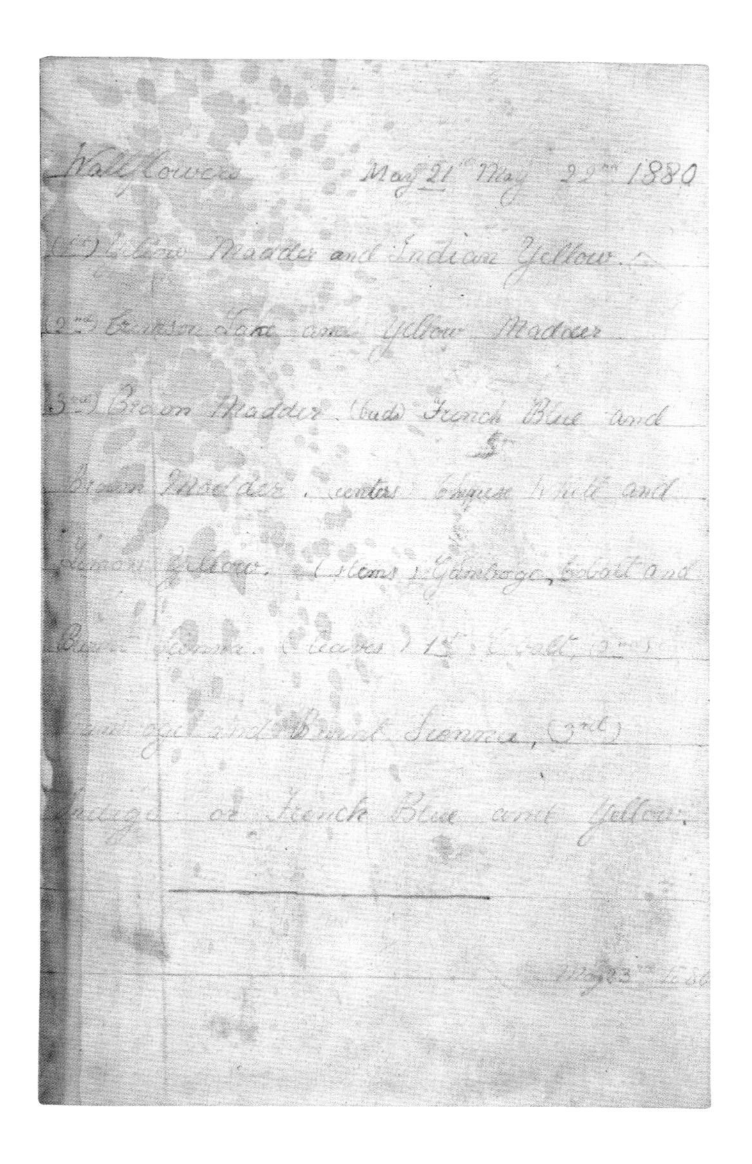

Wallflowers May 21st May 22nd 1880
(1st) Yellow Madder and Indian Yellow.
(2nd) Crimson Lake and Yellow Madder
(3rd) Brown Madder (buds) French Blue and
Brown Madder. centers Chinese White and
Lemon Yellow. (stems) Gamboge, Cobalt and
Brown Sienna. (leaves) 1st Cobalt, 2nd
Gamboge and Burnt Sienna, (3rd)
Indigo or French Blue and Yellow.
May 23rd 1880

Spray of Rose leaves. June 3rd June 4th 1880
(1st lights.) Cobalt, Rose Madder.
(2nd, Cobalt. Indian Yellow.
(3rd) Brown Pink, Cobalt.
4th Crimson Lake. (5th) Brown Madder
Indian Yellow and Rose Madder.
June 3rd
For shading yellow flowers use Emerald
Green and Rose Madder.
Light Hard green. Prussian blue and
Indian Yellow.

Page 1

Wallflowers. May 21st May 22nd 1880
(1st.) Yellow Madder and Indian Yellow.
(2nd.) Crimson Lake and Yellow Madder
(3rd) Brown Madder. (buds) French Blue and Brown Madder.
(centers) [*sic*] Chinese White and Lemon Yellow.
(stems) Gamboge, Cobalt and Burnt Sienna.
(leaves) (1st) Cobalt, (2nd) Gamboge and Burnt Sienna,
(3rd) Indigo or French Blue and Yellow.

Page 3

Spray of Rose leaves. June 3rd. June 4th 1880
(1st.) lights.) [*sic*] Cobalt, Rose Madder.
(2nd, Cobalt, Indian Yellow.
(3rd) Brown Pink. Cobalt.
(4th) Crimson Lake.
(5th) Brown Madder.
[(1st)] Indian Yellow and Rose Madder. June 3rd
For shading yellow flowers use Emerald Green and Rose Madder.
Light. Hard green. Prussian blue and Indian Yellow.

◁ **Sprays of rose leaves, one unfinished**
***June 1880***
Flower painting was one of the accomplishments expected of Victorian girls, but only dedicated young botanists took the trouble to record species and technique. Beatrix Potter's notes from her paintbox drawer refer to a 'Spray of Rose leaves' drawn on June 3rd–4th 1880, when she was not quite fourteen years old.
*Watercolour over pencil*
*image 245x176mm on sheet 317x234mm*
V&A (Linder Bequest)

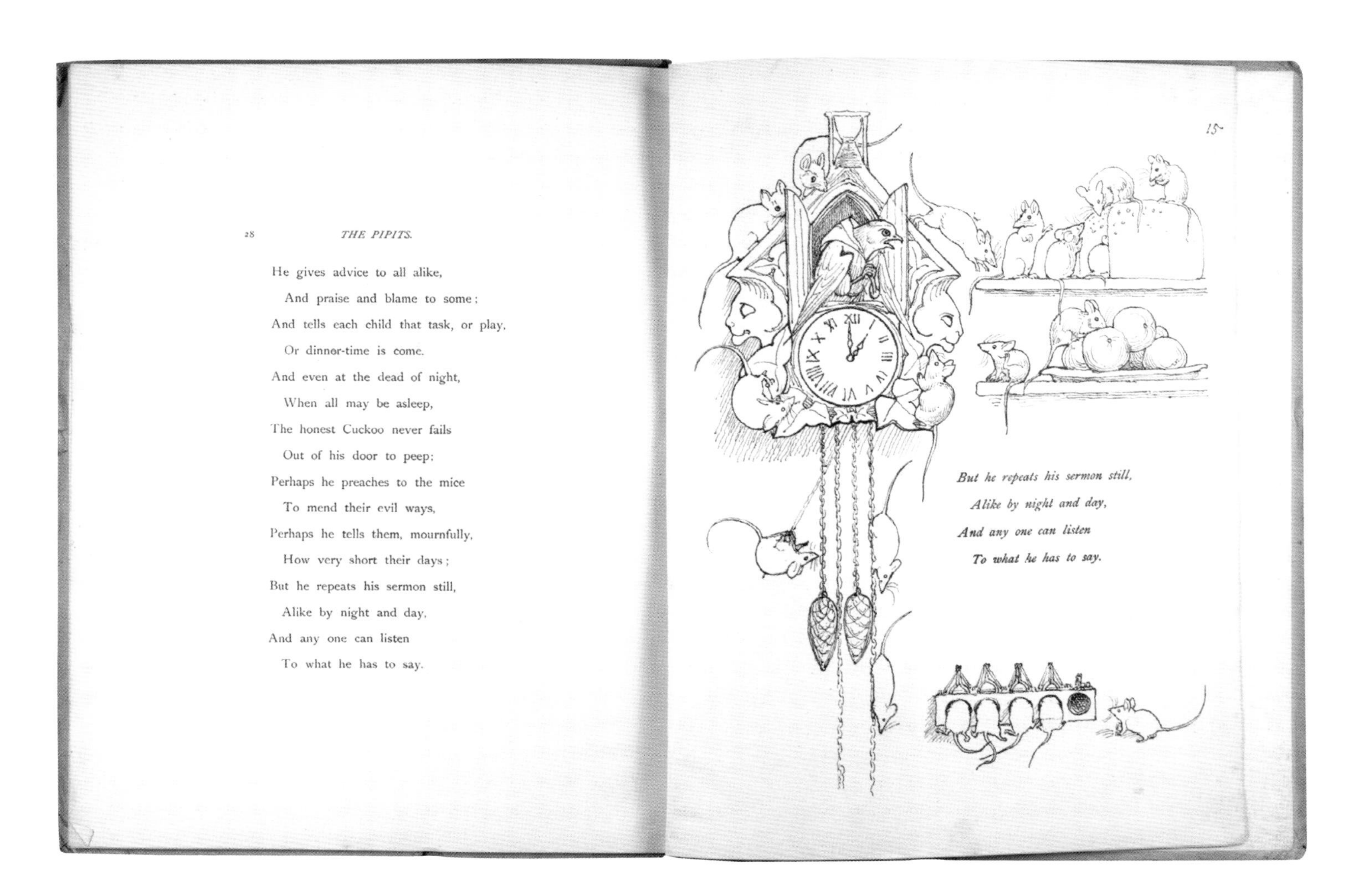

28 THE PIPITS.

He gives advice to all alike,
And praise and blame to some;
And tells each child that task, or play,
Or dinner-time is come.
And even at the dead of night,
When all may be asleep,
The honest Cuckoo never fails
Out of his door to peep;
Perhaps he preaches to the mice
To mend their evil ways,
Perhaps he tells them, mournfully,
How very short their days;
But he repeats his sermon still,
Alike by night and day,
And any one can listen
To what he has to say.

15

*But he repeats his sermon still,*
*Alike by night and day,*
*And any one can listen*
*To what he has to say.*

△ ***The Pipits*, by the author of *'Caw! Caw!'* [Jemima Blackburn]. Glasgow: James Maclehose**
***1872***
'Mrs. Blackburn's birds do not on the average stand on their legs so well as Bewick's, but he is her only possible rival.' Jemima Blackburn, the distinguished Scottish painter and naturalist, illustrated several books for the young; *The Pipits* is one of her narrative bird poems. Beatrix recollected the excitement of being given Blackburn's *Birds Drawn from Nature* on her tenth birthday. She copied the bird paintings in youth and maturity, and in early 1876, these mice running up a clock.
PC

△ **Rabbit at rest**
***1880***
Beatrix Potter's first known rabbit drawings are two tiny pencil outlines in an 1875 drawing book. By 1880 the thirteen-year-old Beatrix was already making serious studies of rabbits. Here she uses feathery brushstrokes, and allows the paper to provide the highlights. Watercolour was a difficult medium for the young artist, but the one she preferred.
*Watercolour over pencil*
*image 96x174mm on sheet 176x252mm*
V&A (Linder Bequest)

'Thank goodness, my education was neglected; I was never sent to school … it would have rubbed off some of the originality.'

**'Roots' of the Peter Rabbit Tales, *Horn Book Magazine* May 1929**

▷ **Studies of a dead deer**

***24 July 1880***

Drawn at Dalguise House, near Dunkeld, just before her fourteenth birthday. Dead or sleeping animals were convenient models: canaries and a siskin, her pet dormouse, and rabbits. Salmon and stags occupy the foreground of photographs taken at Dalguise, a holiday house for eleven consecutive years (1871–1881), where Rupert Potter and visiting friends engaged in country pursuits.

*Watercolour over pencil; pencil*
*images 191x144mm on sheet 256x178mm*

V&A (Linder Bequest)

◁ **Silver cup in neoclassical style**
*[ca. 1885?]*
Inscribed: 'Silver urn, modern copy of old pattern, about 20 inch'. Potter's rendering of its liquid sheen and delicacy expresses her feeling for craftsmanship and form, whether man-made or in nature. Technical aspects interested her, as is evident in a Journal entry (4 November 1881) recording a visit to the silversmiths Hunt and Roskell, where she was shown how such a cup was made.
*Watercolour over pencil*
*image (vignetted) 165x110mm on sheet 229x184mm*
FLP

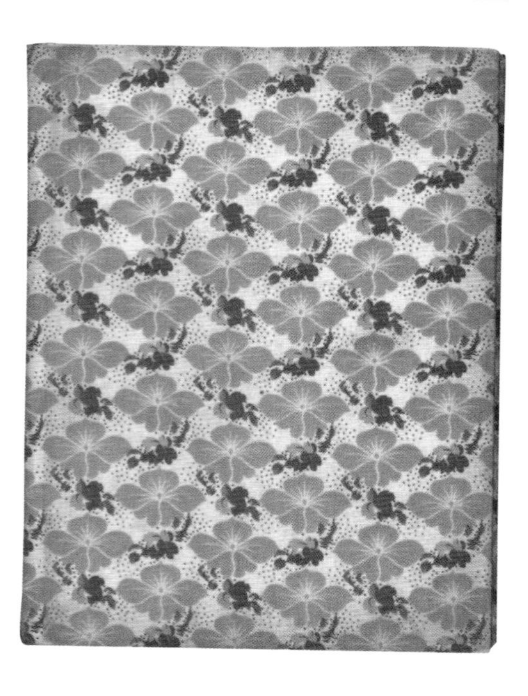

▽ ***The Tale of Squirrel Nutkin, de luxe* edition (second or third printing)**
*1903*
This pansy design was chosen out of several samples sent from the calico printworks at Dinting Vale, Glossop, established in 1824 by Edmund Potter, grandfather of Beatrix. It was used in 1903 for *The Tailor of Gloucester* and *The Tale of Squirrel Nutkin* (but not for the first impression). Other printed cottons may have inspired the clothes of characters in the 'little books'. Dinting Vale also provided scraps of fabric for the portfolios that she constructed to house her most precious drawings, and for the shawl of her Jemima Puddle-duck doll.

Edmund Potter, 'the largest calico printer in the world', an enlightened and much respected employer and a staunch Unitarian, was elected Liberal M.P. for Carlisle, appointed President of the Manchester Art School, and became a Fellow of the Royal Society.
*Printed cotton binding*
*144x107x12mm*
V&A (Linder Bequest)

◁◁ **Place-card decorated with a moth**
*[ca. 1887?]*
For the family, who nicknamed her 'the Busy Bee', Beatrix painted the butterflies and moths that she had studied under the microscope on to little cards. This unidentified specimen was probably copied from a textbook of entomology. Her Christmas card designs made their first appearance at the breakfast table, where they 'proved a five minutes wonder'.
*Watercolour, on card with gold border printed by Marion & Co.*
*image 16x30mm on card 48x85mm*
V&A (Linder Bequest)

△ **Sir John Everett Millais in his studio at 2 Palace Gate, Kensington. Photographed by Rupert Potter**
***18 July 1886***
'I shall always have a most affectionate remembrance of Sir John Millais, though unmercifully afraid of him as a child.' Millais gave Beatrix 'the kindest encouragement' with her drawings, and advised her on the mixing of paints. He once remarked: 'Plenty of people can *draw*, but you … have observation.'
On the wall are two of his paintings: *Lilacs*, and a portrait of Lord Rosebery, the departing Prime Minister.
*Photograph: gelatin silver bromide print*
*159x216mm*
V&A (Linder Bequest)

◁ **'A November day'**
***[ca. 1905]***
Bolton Gardens at dusk, seen from the schoolroom window at No. 2: reminiscent of a twilight painting by Atkinson Grimshaw, or even of Whistler.
*Watercolour over pencil, on board*
*image as sheet 270x183mm*
V&A (Linder Bequest)

▷ **The main staircase at Bedwell Lodge, Hertfordshire**
***October 1891***
Of all the Potter family's holiday houses, the most interesting architecturally and historically was Bedwell Lodge, near Hatfield. A watercolour has recently come to light which depicts the landing above this staircase, and its distinctive Jacobean newel posts.

Staircases and passage-ways provided useful exercises in perspective. Here, reality has been foreshortened for the sake of the composition.
*Watercolour (grey washes) and pen-and-ink over pencil*
*image as sheet 252x161mm*
LT

◁ **'Sunlight & shadow' at Bedwell Lodge**
***August 1891***
An instance of Potter's fascination with the effects of light. Several very similar impressions of this barn interior were done in the course of several days in August and September 1891; one is inscribed 'Sunlight & shadow'. In each version the grouping of the cats remains mysteriously unchanged.
*Watercolour (black and grey monochrome washes) and pen-and-ink over pencil, with highlights in white paint*
*image as sheet 258x161mm*
V&A (Linder Bequest)

▷ **'Mice in their Storeroom'**
***1891***
A study in lighting which shows off Potter's management of space and command of perspective. The back stairs at Bedwell Lodge have been compressed to suit mice; appropriately, sacks of grain and ears of wheat hang on the walls. Familiar houses, already drawn in their own right, supplied settings for the Tales. Bedwell Lodge provided the inspiration for over twenty drawings, and the background for Peter Rabbit's potting shed.
*Watercolour (grey washes) and some pen-and-ink over pencil, with highlights in white paint, pencil frame*
*image 189x148mm on sheet 218x164mm*
V&A (Linder Bequest)

▷ **The back stairs at Bedwell Lodge, Hertfordshire**
***21 September 1891***
Beatrix recorded rooms wherever she stayed, and not just as mementoes. Improved with a panelled passage-way, these back stairs become the setting for 'Mice in their Storeroom'. Several other scenes feature imaginary animals in front of similar panelled backdrops.
*Watercolour (grey washes) and some pen-and-ink over pencil, pen-and-ink partial frame*
*image as sheet 256x162mm*
V&A (Linder Bequest)

# First published work

△ **'Lost Opportunities': greetings card for Hildesheimer & Faulkner**
***[1890]***
The clear colours of the original have become muddied, and Potter's initials have disappeared. The rabbits are now brown; the gentleman wears a sage-green coat and the lady's dress is red; she carries an ermine muff.
*Chromolithograph, on card*
*111x82mm*
BPS

**Rabbits were an important addition** to Beatrix Potter's schoolroom, to her repertoire, and to her career. Driven by the need for £6 towards a printing machine, Beatrix used the handsome Benjamin, her long-eared 'Belgian hare', as model for her first commercial venture: fashionable and profitable greetings cards. (This type of employment was considered suitable for women artists working in miniaturist style.) Learning how to produce the muted tints required by chromolithography, she examined samples expressly cut out of her own card album, and 'toned the colours' from a printed almanac. Only in this early work, done to order, is there any hint of the saccharine; she later remarked, 'I never liked those cards.'

Some of Potter's best designs occurred to her in chapel; six of them were accepted by the firm of Hildesheimer & Faulkner in May 1890. Mr. Faulkner was more concerned with humour than with likeness, as her Journal records. 'Not one word did he say in praise of the cards, but he showed a mysterious desire for more. ... His one idea seemed to me to be fiddles and trousers. Now, if there is anything hideous, it is trousers, but I have conceded them in two guinea-pig drawings' (*see pages* 78–9). For Ernest Nister and Co. she produced the successful pictorial sequence 'A Frog he would a-fishing go', but not before they had haggled over the price.

Potter exploited her own popularity for the benefit of charity. She reused early card designs for the Invalid Children's Aid Association (now I CAN) from 1925 to 1941, two years before her death.

▷ **'Lost Opportunities': watercolour and preparatory outline drawing**
***June 1890***

The optimistic gentleman carries a sprig of mistletoe, but the lady passes by. Rabbits and costumes changed colour for both printed card and booklet. Variant designs depict the white rabbits with blue and brown coats, and a long-skirted coat for the gentleman.

*Watercolour, with traces of metallic paint, and pen-and-ink; pen-and-ink over pencil with some corrections in white paint*
*images (vignetted) 115x76mm on sheet 177x115mm, 108x87mm on sheet 168x106mm*
LT

◁ **Benjamin Bunny in eighteenth-century dress**
***1890***

Probably intended for a greetings card, this is the finished version of a pen-and-ink design now in the Linder Bequest. An elegant Benjamin is dressed in the style of the Gentleman Mouse from *The Tailor of Gloucester*, complete with tricorne hat; the bow stitched to the back of his coat collar represents a bag wig. Potter adopted archaizing costumes for all her greetings card designs and some of the Tales. Eighteenth-century clothes from the Victoria and Albert Museum were so accurately drawn that they can be identified today.

*Watercolour and pen-and-ink*
*image (vignetted) 74x57mm on sheet 250x210mm*
PC

◁ ***A Happy Pair*, by Frederic E. Weatherly. London: Hildesheimer & Faulkner (printed in Germany)**
***[1890]***

Potter's canny publishers instantly repackaged her cards in a little Christmas booklet, accompanied by specially written verses. The author was a prolific Victorian songwriter and barrister.

*Chromolithograph on cover, with silk tasselled cord*
*120x100mm*
V&A (Linder Bequest)

▷ **Mother guinea pig with soup tureen, chased by three young (scene 1)**
*[1890?]*
The inscription shows Potter's intentions: 'Piebald guinea pigs – , black jackets, grey trousers –' The publisher ignored her instruction: on the printed cards the jackets are dark blue.
*Pen-and-ink over pencil*
*image (vignetted) 46x161mm on sheet 138x205mm*
LT

▽ **Five guinea pigs at table (scene 2)**
*[1890?]*
No intermediate, watercolour stage is known for this pair of designs, which may explain the pronounced difference between original concept and finished product: in colour and relative size, and in the head and eyes of the parent guinea pig.
*Pen-and-ink over erased pencil, with some corrections in white paint*
*image (vignetted) 52x163mm on sheet 135x204mm*
PC

△ △ **Pair of guinea pig greetings cards for Hildesheimer & Faulkner**
***[1890?]***
These designs were reused in *Our Dear Relations*, published by Hildesheimer & Faulkner [*ca.* 1893?], again with verses by F. E. Weatherly. Both the first scene, with a Christmas greeting, and its New Year sequel, have an unpleasant glossy smoothness.
*Chromolithographs, on card*
*images (vignetted) 55x120mm on sheet 88x131mm, 62x121mm on sheet 89x132mm*
V&A (Linder Bequest)

▷ **'Jackdaw Sweep'**
***[1892]***
'I was busy in the morning finishing a drawing of a Jackdaw for Nister & Co. for which, by the way, they have not paid' (*Journal*, 30 July 1892); nor did they print it. Potter's correspondence with this 'unattractive' Bavarian firm reveals her as a tough-minded businesswoman.
*Watercolour over pencil, with some highlights in white paint*
*image (vignetted) 67x66mm on sheet 163x124mm*
V&A (Linder Bequest)

◁ **Two gentlemen rabbits in the snow**
***[1894]***
Originally intended for a Christmas card; an almost identical drawing was given to the children of Annie Moore, Beatrix Potter's last governess. This version was pulled from the portfolios to serve as the frontispiece for *Appley Dapply's Nursery Rhymes* (1917).

A fine brush (or 'pencil') made it possible to produce minute and exquisite detail, enhanced by touches of red in cuffs and muffler. The rustic fence, a favourite motif, appears in several greetings card backgrounds.
*Watercolour over erased pencil; initials masked in white paint*
*image (vignetted) 83x52mm on sheet 144x128mm*
NT

◁ **'December': design used in *Peter Rabbit's Almanac for 1929***
***[1892?]***
Publication of this almanac was postponed, because Beatrix, preoccupied with the lambing season, was also finding close work a strain on her eyes. Many of the illustrations had been done years earlier as greetings card designs, with favourite themes of rabbits in snowy doorways, on sledges, and gathering firewood. Others were reused in the 1930s for charity Christmas cards.
*Watercolour over erased pencil*
*image (vignetted) 82x58mm on sheet 141x127mm*
NT

# Fantasy and humour

▷ **'The Squirrel's Gift'**
*[ca. 1895]*
A picture that tells a story, combining imaginative and naturalistic detail. Small brushstrokes produce a sculptural effect, emphasized by white highlights on the squirrel's tail. Around this time Beatrix was exploring the surprising tonal variety achievable within a limited colour range of grey washes.
*Watercolour (grey washes) and pen-and-ink over pencil, with highlights in white paint, watercolour frame*
*image 187x138mm on sheet 222x173mm*
V&A (Linder Bequest)

◁ **'Peter's dream of a comfortable bed' ('The Rabbit's Dream')**
*[1899?]*
One of four known versions of 'The Rabbit's Dream', with varying numbers of rabbits, all dating from 1895 to 1899. Sleep and dream are recurring themes in Victorian art, and in Potter's art as well. Peter dreams in No. 4 bedroom, Camfield Place, where Beatrix slept when visiting her paternal grandparents.

The investigative naturalist uses her knowledge with wit. Peter is framed by studies of sleeping rabbits, just as the border of an *Uncle Remus* design records the various attitudes of rabbits in action.
*Pen-and-ink over pencil, with corrections in white paint*
*image 196x185mm on sheet 314x208mm*
V&A (Linder Bequest)

▷ **Alphabet designs**
*[ca. 1895?]*
Beatrix Potter knew just what would amuse her young cousins and child friends: specially constructed 'toy pictures' with movable parts, and letters of the alphabet made fun – chewed and roosted in by mice and rabbits, or used as an umbrella.
*Pencil*
*images 162x82mm on sheet 202x125mm*
V&A (Linder Bequest)

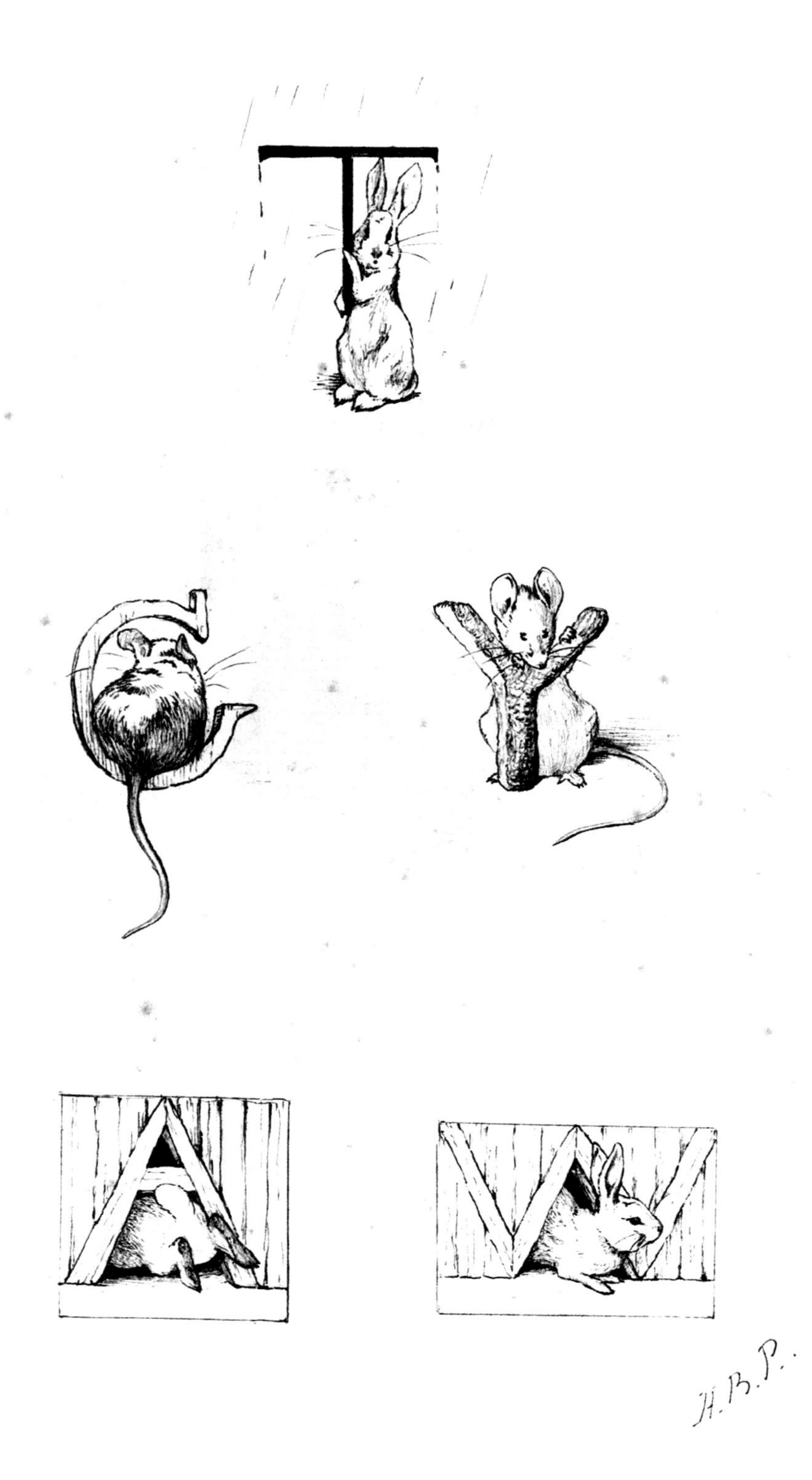

◁ **'Dicky's Cake Dance'**
***20 December 1900***

Sugar bowl and tongs, cream jug, tea-pot and plates cavort round a birthday cake with coloured candles; knives bow low among the dancing holly leaves and mistletoe. White highlighting brings out the gleam of sprightly sugar lumps and the icing on the cake. The receding curve of the railway track gives depth to the design.

Beatrix Potter made a tracing of this picture to keep for herself, since she gave it away as a fourth birthday present for her young cousin Richard Mallet, grandson of Sir Henry Roscoe.

*Watercolour and pen-and-ink over erased pencil, with highlights in white paint*
*image 318x256mm on sheet 355x287mm*
PC

▷ **'The peculiar DREAM of Mr. Samuel Whiskers, upon the subject of DUTCH CHEESE'**
***[ca. 1903?]***

This rather uncharacteristic palette of translucent pinks and blues is found in only a few other paintings by Potter. The title, lettered in whimsically formal style, parodies eighteenth-century prose. Beatrix wrote on the back: 'Studies of a tame white rat "Sammy" – from life'. Dedicatee of *The Roly-Poly Pudding*, that story about undesirable elements of society, Sammy is apostrophized as 'an affectionate little Friend, and a most accomplished Thief'.

*Watercolour and pen-and-ink over pencil; inscription in ink*
*image (vignetted) 252x200mm on sheet 284x216mm*
V&A (Linder Bequest)

The peculiar DREAM of Mr Samuel Whiskers, upon the subject of DUTCH CHEESE -

# ILLUSTRATIONS

**The Victorian era saw a revival of interest in folklore,** as newly translated tales flooded into England. For pleasure and practice, and as a diversion from natural history, Beatrix Potter enjoyed the challenge of illustrating already much-illustrated texts and classic authors: fairy tales, fables and rhymes, *Uncle Remus,* Lewis Carroll and Edward Lear. Designs by Otto Speckter and Ludwig Richter served as models for practice in architectural and figure drawing, but she added her own modishly asymmetrical borders, in an over-decorated style which she later abandoned. Though some of her illustrations are Germanic in style, most were original in concept. She preferred the more congenial episodes involving animals, plants or landscapes, and her animals were drawn from life.

Accomplished but idiosyncratic designs for *Alice* and *Uncle Remus* were pursued no further and never published. Once established as author-illustrator, Potter resisted the suggestion that she might illustrate other people's books, and it is as her own interpreter that she is most in sympathy with the text.

'With regard to illustrating other people's books, I have a strong feeling that every outside book which I did, would prevent me from finishing one of my own.'

**21 February 1904, to Norman Warne**

## Lewis Carroll

**Two designs for *Alice's Adventures in Wonderland* *[1893?]***

**△ 'The White Rabbit, splendidly dressed'**
An albino Peter in his blue jacket, but an unmistakable White Rabbit in his attitude.

**▷ 'The Rabbit started violently ... & skurried *[sic]* away into the darkness as hard as he could go'**
An atmosphere of nightmare is evoked by the claustrophobically narrow receding corridor.
*Watercolour and pen-and-ink over pencil, pencil frames*
*images each 84x70mm on sheets 108x92mm and 107x91mm, mounted together on card 214x278mm*
LT

◁▽ **The White Rabbit: two unfinished designs for *Alice's Adventures in Wonderland* *[1893?]***

'Dickens, and Alice-in-Wonderland, have been illustrated once for all,' Potter wrote in 1927, but she had long since joined the ranks of Carroll illustrators. Her six or seven *Alice* designs vary considerably in style, and do not form a set. Unlike Tenniel the caricaturist, she avoids human subjects.

*Watercolour and pen-and-ink over pencil, pencil frames*

*images 103x75mm on sheet 168x109mm, 89x73mm on sheet 166x99mm*

V&A (Linder Bequest)

## Uncle Remus

▷ **'Brer Fox he look at Brer Rabbit', for 'Mr. Fox goes a-Hunting'** ***(Uncle Remus: his Songs and his Sayings, 1880)***
***November 1895***
These subversive African stories in an American setting were recorded by Joel Chandler Harris. Their shrewd humour and virtuosity of language appealed to Beatrix Potter, with her sensitivity to tone of voice and fondness for dialect. Peter Piper, her pet rabbit, modelled for nine illustrations dated between 1893 and early 1896. For the first scene she drew a variant version; this is the only episode for which she made two designs, in the same month. There are echoes of *Uncle Remus* in her own books: 'Cotton-tail' and the Black Rabbit, 'lippity-lippity' and rabbit tobacco, and the plot of *Mr. Tod*. The fir tree in this picture reappears in *The Tale of Peter Rabbit*.

Asymmetric partial borders in the Art Nouveau or Japanese manner were fashionable at the time. Here, the border motif reinforces the narrative moment, so that two consecutive episodes are simultaneously shown.
*Pencil (primary image); pen-and-ink (border image)*
*total image 251x174mm on sheet 279x216mm; primary image 178x141mm on sheet 190x141mm*
V&A (Linder Bequest)

## Fairy tales

**◁△ Kittens collect game for the White Cat's supper: two designs**
***1894***
'The White Cat', a fairy tale by the Countess d'Aulnoy (d. 1705), is set in a Hertfordshire landscape. Sporting prints may have inspired these kittens with guns and game-bag; their clothing is unaccountably inconsistent. A third scene, with only one kitten, was published in a Nister booklet. Neckerchief, roofs and foreground foliage provide the essential dash of red.
*Watercolour and pen-and-ink*
*images (vignetted) 102x78mm on sheet 173x121mm, 112x74mm on sheet 173x120mm*
V&A (Linder Bequest)

△ **'Cinderella's carriage going to fetch her from the ball, intended for *moon*light'**
***[1899?]***
A tinted ground, in combination with various shades of grey, gives the illusion of moonlight, and format is suited to subject.

Each of the three known versions of this design has a slightly different combination of creatures; one includes stag-beetles. The backdrop is reminiscent of mediaeval Gloucester.
*Watercolour (grey washes) and pen-and-ink over pencil, on cream-tinted board*
*image as sheet 139x278mm.*
V&A (Linder Bequest)

# NARRATIVE SEQUENCES

**Every fantasy picture by Beatrix Potter 'tells a story',** but her real flair was for pictorial narrative. Simple linear tales unfold like strip-cartoons: wordless, or with apt and pithy commentary. Her earliest known sequence dates from November 1888; its three instalments record the encounter of a shrew and a fly. There follow a picture story about a guinea pig with toothache, and several versions of 'The Owl and the Pussy Cat'. Nursery rhymes lent themselves to multi-episodic treatment too: 'Three Little Mice', and 'Appley Dapply', 'This little pig', and 'The old woman who lived in a shoe' (*see pages 118–29*). Caldecott's economy of line and sense of space inspired 'A Frog he would a-fishing go' (1894), and *The Sly Old Cat.*

**'Three Little Mice sat down to spin'**
***[ca. 1892]***
One of several ideas for illustrated booklets, planned but never published. This sequence reached an advanced stage of preparation; a concertina format may have been envisaged, with pictures on front and back in the style of *A Happy Pair*. As with other work being prepared for publication (*see* 'Lost Opportunities', *pages 74–5*), detailed pen-and-ink outlines served as a guide for painting. The fourth design was adapted for *The Tailor of Gloucester* (page 45), but the rhyme itself appears only in the privately printed edition.

Beatrix Potter's familiarity with the textile industry supplied the industrial weaving shuttle, but the mice are using cottagers' looms; their spinning wheels were apparently drawn from incomplete examples. Bentwood chairs commemorate one from bedroom 'No. 4 where I always slept' at her grandparents' home, Camfield Place.
*Watercolour and pen-and-ink over erased pencil, with some white paint, some pencil frames, mounted on card*

◁ **Three little Mice sat down to spin**
*image 87x128mm on sheet 98x139mm*
▷ **Pussy passed by, and she peeped in**
*image 88x128mm on sheet 96x138mm*
**'What are you at, my fine little Men?'**
*image 89x128mm on sheet 98x139mm*
**'Making coats for Gentlemen'**
*image 89x128mm on sheet 97x139mm*
**'Shall I come in, and cut off your threads?'**
*image 87x127mm on sheet 97x138mm*
**'Oh no! Miss Pussy, you'd bite off our heads'**
*image 89x128mm on sheet 99x139mm*

▷▷ **Design for the front cover**
An asymmetrical layout fashionable at this period.
*image 60x91mm on sheet 97x140mm*
**Design for the back cover**
A coloured version of the fifth line drawing, but with a slightly different arrangement of objects.
*image (vignetted) 28x115mm on sheet 101x165mm*
**Text pages**
Below each line of text are sepia drawings of domestic articles, chronologically arranged: spinning tools and weaving apparatus, then writing and sewing utensils, ending aptly with padlock, keys and candle-snuffer.
*Sepia ink over erased pencil; text in pencil with ruled lines*
*images 20x112mm, 41x117mm, 27x114mm, 29x112mm, 20x111mm, 32x107mm, each on sheet ca. 102x165mm*
V&A (Linder Bequest)

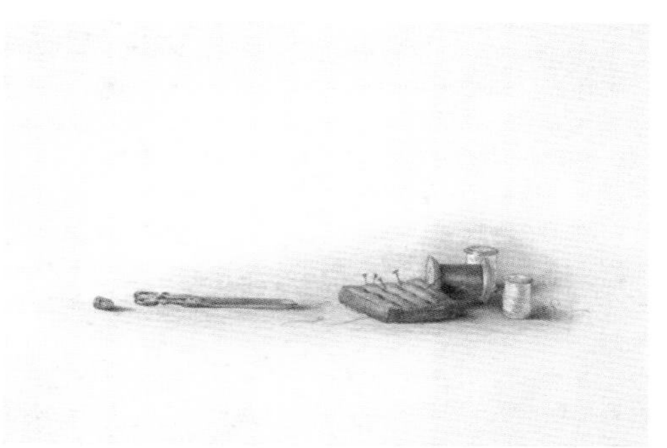

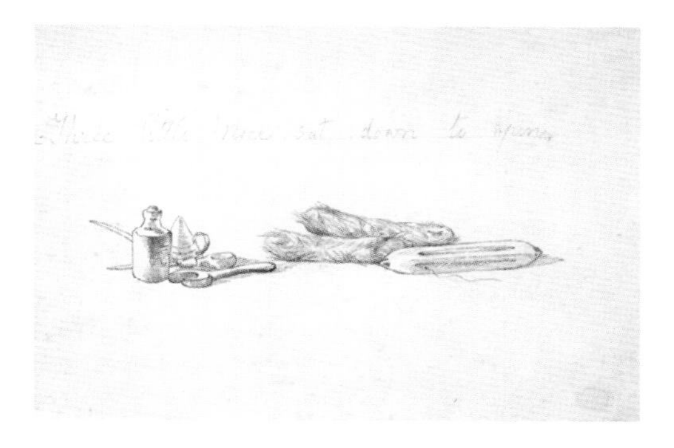

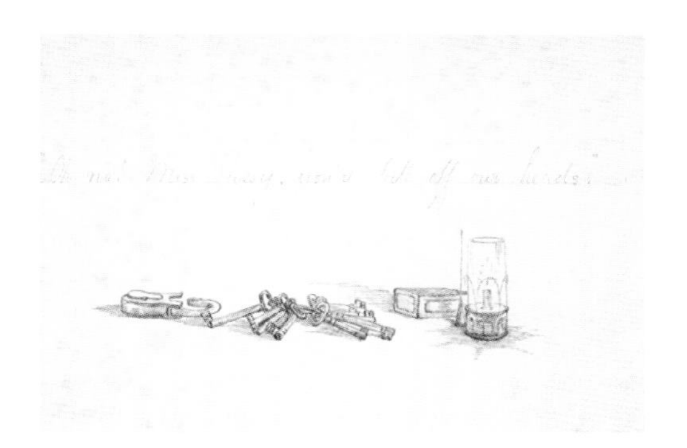

**'The Rabbits' Christmas Party'**
***[1892?]***

Beatrix presented this set of four paintings to her aunt Lucy Roscoe, wife of 'Uncle Harry', an enterprising woman who took up photography even earlier than did her better-known brother Rupert Potter, the father of Beatrix. An extra pair of scenes, in which the rabbits dance to a piper and play Blind Man's Buff, was given to Henry P. Coolidge of Boston, USA, in 1927. 'The Arrival' is uncannily reminiscent of Renoir's *Les Parapluies*, which Beatrix is however unlikely to have seen.

The attitudes are both rabbit-like and human. Only an artist with an intimate knowledge of anatomy could convey so well both musculature and the texture of fur. Remarkable, as in all Potter's animal drawing, is her observation of ears.

*Watercolour and pen-and-ink, with highlights and corrections in white paint, pencil frames, initials in ink over pencil, scenes 2-4 numbered on versos, mounted on card*

V&A (Linder Bequest)

△△ **The Arrival**
*image 150x150mm on sheet 161x ca.158mm*
△ **Christmas Dinner**
*image 152x153mm on sheet 160x163mm*
◁ **Roasting Apples**
*image 150x150mm on sheet 153x158mm*
▽ **The Departure**
*image 154x151mm on sheet ca. 163x161mm*

▷ 'July': design used in *Peter Rabbit's Almanac for 1929*
*[1917?]*
The *Almanac*, like the two rhyme books, was 'a way of using up odds and ends': a compilation of early drawings reworked and later additions such as this example, with its by now woollier line. 'July' corresponds to one of the two scenes added to the 'Rabbits' Christmas Party' sequence, but has two rabbits fewer, and its setting is a burrow.
*Watercolour over pencil*
*image (vignetted) 78x60mm on sheet 168x98mm*
NT

▷ Questing mouse: unused illustration for *The Story of Miss Moppet*
*[1906]*
A design printed in monochrome, much reduced, on the title page of the concertina edition, and left out of the standard book-format edition which replaced it. Only a few preliminary drawings survive for this story, and a panoramic manuscript in pencil.
*Watercolour and sepia ink or paint*
*image 45x50mm on sheet 80x77mm*
PC

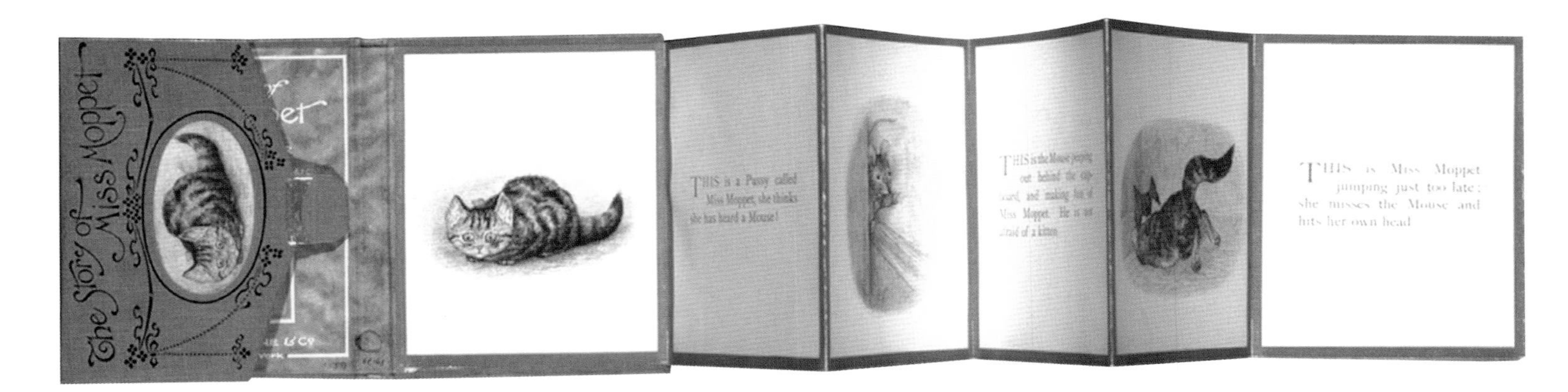

◁ ***The Story of Miss Moppet*: panoramic edition**
***1906***
Beatrix Potter's two published panoramas were planned with alternating illustration and text, a picture on the cover, and another in tone inside. Texts were short and plain, and the plots kept simple.

The kitten with the ribbon had made her début in print on a first edition cover for *The Pie and the Patty-Pan*, and several years before in a little card design for Ernest Nister. Modelled on the mason's cat from Windermere, she was 'very young & pretty and a most fearful pickle'.
*108x2492mm (108x89mm folded); 15 spreads*
PC

She ties him up in the duster, and tosses it about like a ball.

But she forgot about that hole in the duster; and when she untied it – there was no Mouse!

He has wriggled out and run away; and he is dancing a jig on top of the cupboard!

('The Story of Miss Moppet' by Beatrix Potter)

◁ **'He is dancing a jig on the top of the cupboard!': cartoon by Nicholas Garland after Beatrix Potter, *The Daily Telegraph***
***18 December 2003***
Michael Howard teases Tony Blair, but Blair gives Howard the slip – again.

*The Story of Miss Moppet* is 'a solid pile of political cartoons waiting to happen ... Beatrix Potter's tales are filled with scenes and characters that can be used by the cartoonist.' (Garland, 1993)
*Pen-and-ink and wash*
*image 255x380mm*
PC

▷ ***The Story of A Fierce Bad Rabbit*: panoramic manuscript**
***[February? 1906]***

The first manuscript of *A Fierce Bad Rabbit*, mounted on green linen and specially bound with a silver clasp, was presented to Harold Warne's older daughter for her sixth birthday. Two other manuscripts are known, one dated 23 February 1906. Louie Warne had asked for a story about a naughtier rabbit than Peter; it was published in November in a binding that copied the original wallet style but was inconvenient and easily damaged. Both *Miss Moppet* and *A Fierce Bad Rabbit* were withdrawn, and reissued in book format in 1916.

For the new edition, Beatrix (by now Mrs. Heelis) promised, but failed, to make a correction. Her husband had pointed out that the gun was not held properly.

*Watercolour and pen-and-ink over pencil; text in ink, with suggested amendments in faint pencil*
*118x2875mm (118x102mm folded); images each ca. 75x75mm; 15 spreads*
NT

▷ **'He comes creeping up behind the trees': cartoon by Nicholas Garland after Beatrix Potter, *The Daily Telegraph***
***19 September 2002***

Dramatic tension and strong characterization are present in *The Story of A Fierce Bad Rabbit*, although story and pictures are weaker than in the other two panoramas. There is scope for the cartoonist: all those occasions when politicians make trouble 'by seizing the initiative (the carrot) from their leaders or colleagues'.

William Heelis was a keen shot, but Beatrix Potter insisted that 'hunting by otter hounds and harriers shall be forbidden and prohibited over the whole of my Troutbeck property'.

*Pen-and-ink and wash, white paint 'frame'*
*image 282x390mm*
PC

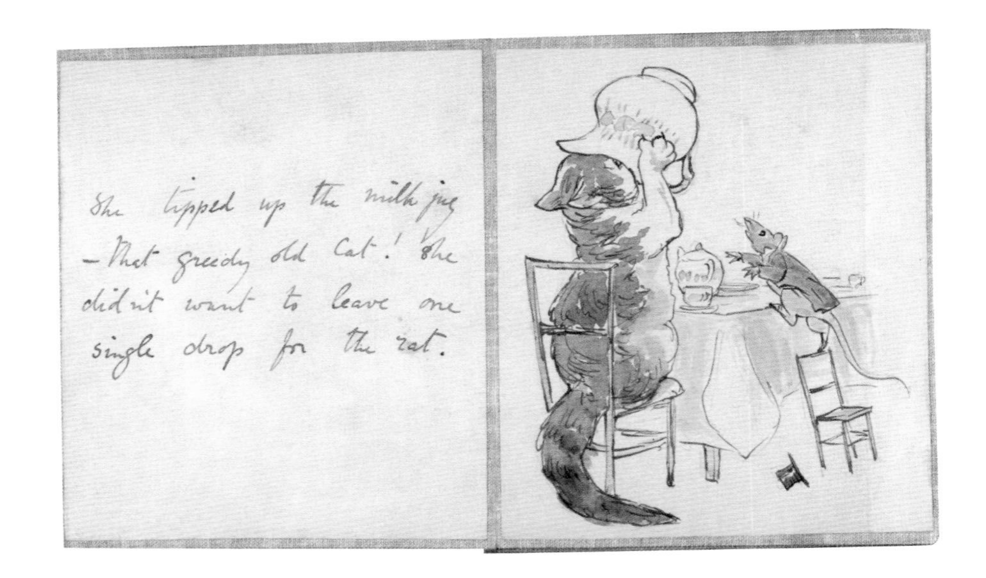

◁▷ **'The Sly Old Cat': panoramic manuscript**
***20 March 1906***

The twenty-fourth Tale, third of a trio of concertina books for very young children, was planned for 1907 but cancelled, because shopkeepers were reluctant to stock such fragile objects. It was advertised in a 1916 endpaper as *The Story of The Sly Old Cat*, only to disappear again until its eventual publication in 1971, in standard book format.

'Nellie's little rat story' was presented to Harold Warne's younger daughter and specially bound for her by the firm, mounted on blue cloth instead of green. Since the illustrations were never prepared for publication, the colour is unfinished and still subservient to the line, which has lost nothing of its spontaneity. The tale is told, with hidden rhyme, in words of one syllable used with economy and deceptive simplicity. Narrative flow is accelerated by format, and though the text can stand alone, this is a perfect marriage of word and image.

*Watercolour and sepia ink over erased pencil; text in sepia ink*
*112x2798mm (117x100mm folded); images each 105x90mm; 14 spreads*
V&A (Linder Bequest)

▽ **'A Frog he would a-wooing go', from R. Caldecott's *Second Collection of Pictures and Songs* (pages 20-21). London: George Routledge and Sons**
***[1885]***
Caldecott's figures leap out of the page. Some of Potter's designs have the same dramatic, centrifugal energy.
PC

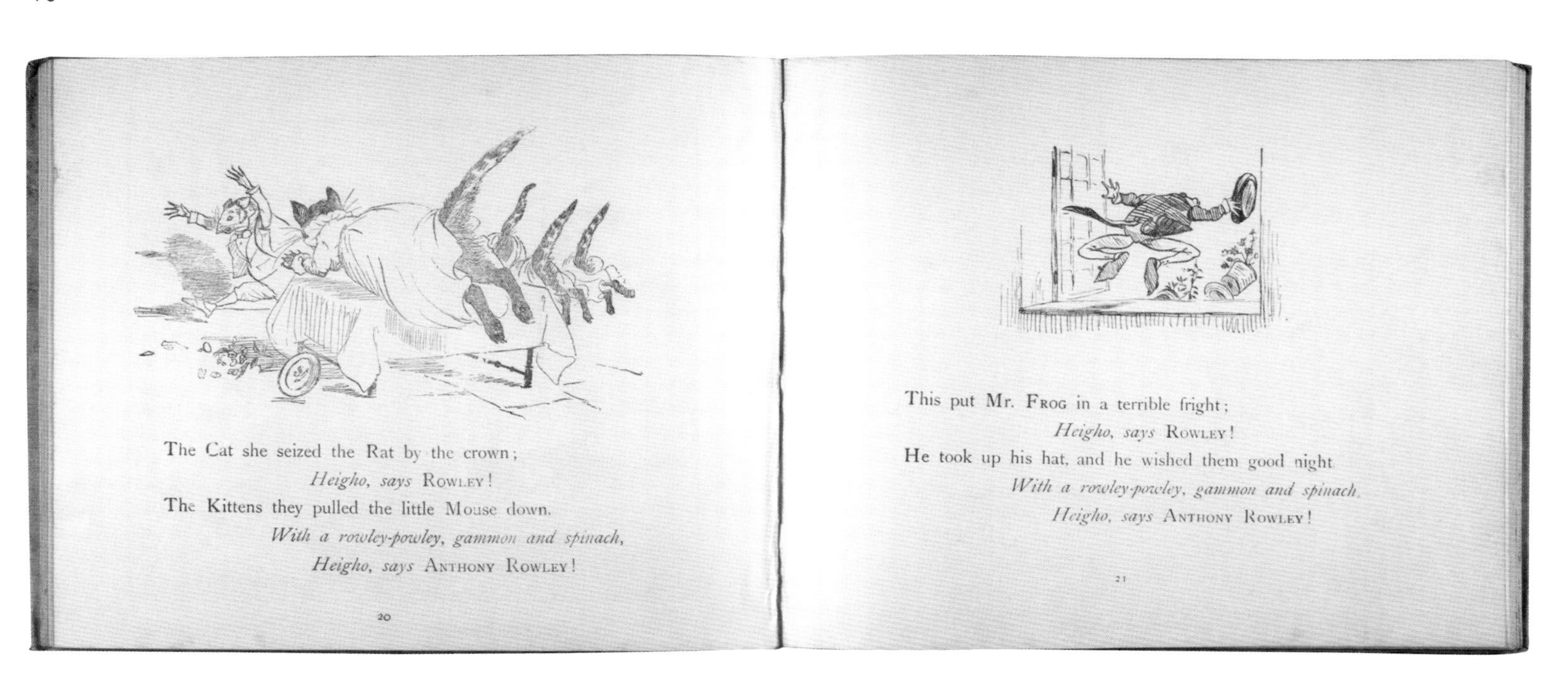
The Cat she seized the Rat by the crown;
*Heigho, says* Rowley!
The Kittens they pulled the little Mouse down.
*With a rowley-powley, gammon and spinach,*
*Heigho, says* Anthony Rowley!

20

This put Mr. Frog in a terrible fright;
*Heigho, says* Rowley!
He took up his hat, and he wished them good night
*With a rowley-powley, gammon and spinach,*
*Heigho, says* Anthony Rowley!

21

# THE BOOKS AND THEIR BACKGROUNDS

## The little books

**Beatrix Potter's gifts for visual and verbal story-telling were equally matched:** a rare combination. Amusing and action-packed illustrated letters to child friends provided source-material; a few were actual tales in embryo. Their success with children and adults alike gave her the confidence to take her own books into print with entrepreneurial determination.

By 1894 there was a vogue for small books, such as *The Temple Shakespeare* and *The Dumpy Books for Children* which included *The Tale of Little Black Sambo* (1899). Potter, with her customary acumen, and her sense of what was aesthetically appropriate as well as practical, felt that children's books should be small and inexpensive, and 'made to fit little hands'. Originally, however, the books were uniform neither in size nor in method of illustration - and no two tipped-on cover labels are the same. Experiments were made with a larger format for three of the titles, but later all were reduced to standard size, including both published panoramas. The rhyme books were shorter and slimmer; *The Tale of Mr. Tod* (1912) was the first of a 'New Series', thicker and with a more elaborate binding; and the last of the Tales, *Little Pig Robinson*, was considerably larger, modelled on *The Fairy Caravan*.

At Potter's insistence, the books exploited the new three-colour printing process, more expensive than wood-block printing but better suited to the reproduction of her watercolours, in spite of the glossy 'clay faced' paper it required. She drew a large number of variant pictures, often because the publishers asked for new compositions – not always an improvement – in which the figures were more prominent in relation to their background.

During twelve fruitful years between 1901 and her marriage in 1913, Beatrix Potter produced nineteen of the twenty-three 'Tales'. Afterwards, there were few works of the same calibre. Described as 'one of the best prose stylists of the century' (P. Parker), her influence has been acknowledged by W. H. Auden and Christopher Isherwood, Sir Steven Runciman and Graham Greene.

***The 23 'Original Peter Rabbit Books'***

*The Tale of Peter Rabbit 1902*
*The Tale of Squirrel Nutkin 1903*
*The Tailor of Gloucester 1903*
*The Tale of Benjamin Bunny 1904*
*The Tale of Two Bad Mice 1904*
*The Tale of Mrs. Tiggy-Winkle 1905*
*The Tale of The Pie and The Patty-Pan 1905*
*The Tale of Mr. Jeremy Fisher 1906*
*The Story of A Fierce Bad Rabbit 1906*
*The Story of Miss Moppet 1906*
*The Tale of Tom Kitten 1907*
*The Tale of Jemima Puddle-Duck 1908*
*The Tale of Samuel Whiskers or The Roly-Poly Pudding 1908*
*The Tale of The Flopsy Bunnies 1909*
*The Tale of Ginger and Pickles 1909*
*The Tale of Mrs. Tittlemouse 1910*
*The Tale of Timmy Tiptoes 1911*
*The Tale of Mr. Tod 1912*
*The Tale of Pigling Bland 1913*
*Appley Dapply's Nursery Rhymes 1917*
*The Tale of Johnny Town-Mouse 1918*
*Cecily Parsley's Nursery Rhymes 1922*
*The Tale of Little Pig Robinson 1930*

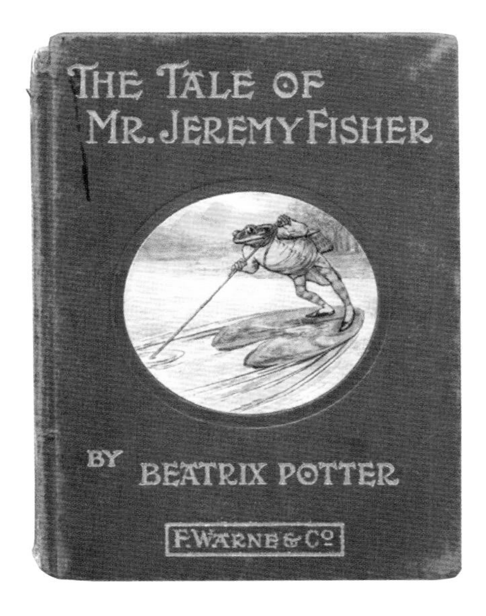


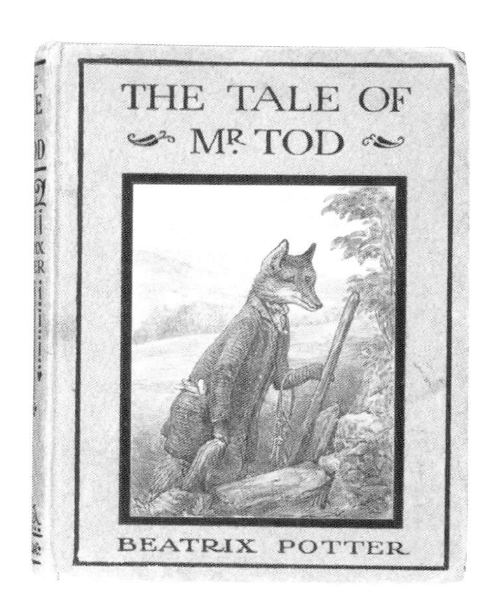

△ *The Tale of Peter Rabbit* 1 trade ed
***1902***
*dark brown boards; 143x107mm*
WA
△ △ *The Tale of Mr. Jeremy Fisher* 1 ed
***1906***
*crimson boards; 143x106mm*
WA
△ △ △ *The Tale of Mr. Tod* 1 ed
***October or November 1912***
*grey boards; 143x112mm*
WA
▷ *The Pie and the Patty-Pan* 1 ed
***October 1905***
*blue boards (kitten in roundel); 182x142mm*
WA

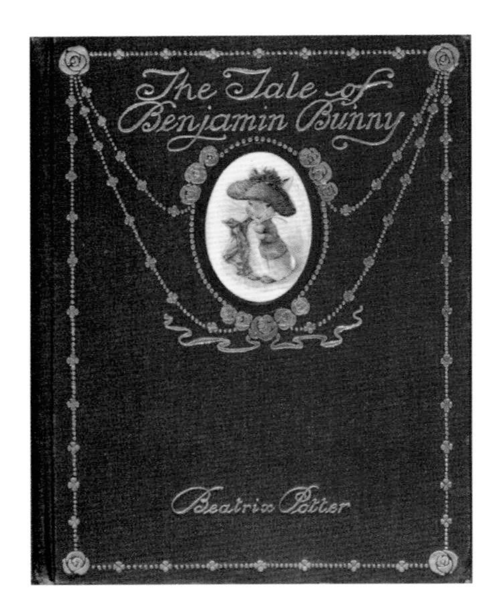

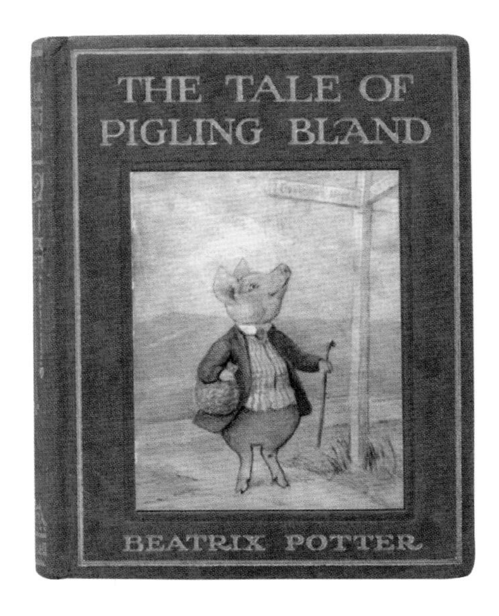


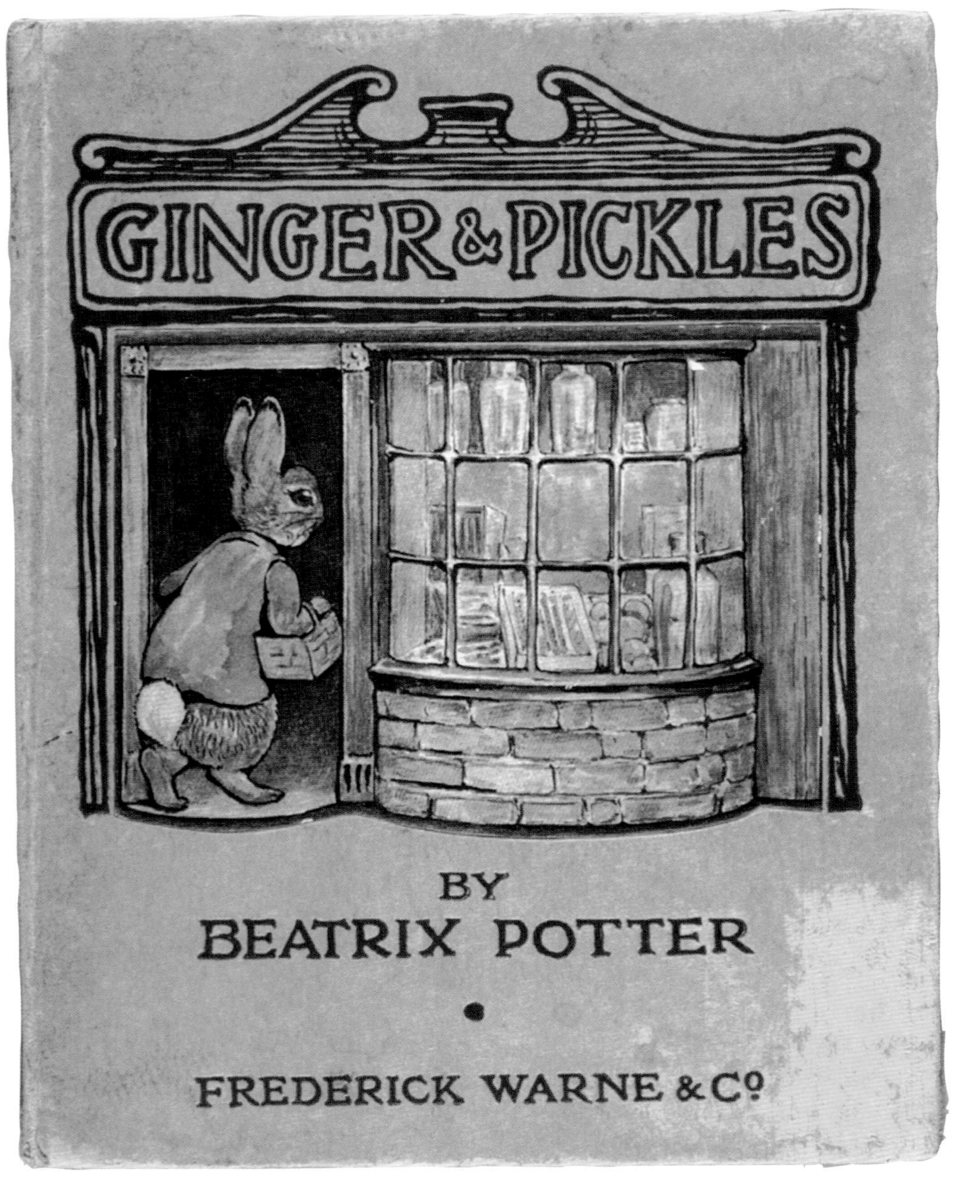


△ ***The Tale of Pigling Bland*** **1 ed**
***October or November 1913***
*maroon boards; 143x110mm*
WA

△△ ***The Tailor of Gloucester*** **1 ed, *de luxe***
***1903***
*art fabric (pansy design); 142x109mm*
WA

△△△ ***The Tale of Benjamin Bunny*** **1 ed, *de luxe***
***September or October 1904***
*blue decorated cloth; 143x108mm*
WA

◁ ***Ginger and Pickles*** **1 ed**
***October or November 1909***
*beige boards; 182x141mm*
WA

## The Tale of Peter Rabbit

▷ **'Your Father ... was put in a pie by Mrs. McGregor'**
*[1902]*
Human subjects were not Beatrix Potter's forte; her brother was 'sarcastic about the figures'. A middle-aged Mrs. McGregor, included in the privately printed edition, was rejected by the publisher as too frightening for children. Norman Warne commented, in red ink: 'We still do not like the old woman's face. Will you please have another try at this.' It was replaced by a poor drawing, with added child, of an incongruously young but less frightening Mrs. McGregor (a self-portrait), but this too was soon withdrawn as too gruesome a reminder of rabbit pie.
*Watercolour and pen-and-ink*
*image 58x84mm on sheet 205x122mm*
V&A (Linder Bequest)

▷ **Two rabbits nibbling a turnip**
*[ca. 1895?]*
Drawings from the 1880s and 1890s provided source-material for Beatrix Potter's books: this bird turns up again in *The Tale of Peter Rabbit*, as one of the three sparrow guides who implore Peter to exert himself. The panelling and stone-flagged floor appear in several contemporary rhyme illustrations and greetings card designs.
*Pencil, pencil frame, on tinted paper*
*image 189x139mm on sheet 250x177mm*
V&A (Linder Bequest)

'We still do not like the old woman's face.'

**Norman Warne 1902**

**Three line illustrations from the privately printed *Tale of Peter Rabbit***
***December 1901; February 1902***

*The Tale of Peter Rabbit*, first and best-known of Potter's twenty-three Tales, originates in an illustrated letter sent on 4 September 1893 to a sick boy, Noël Moore, oldest child of Beatrix Potter's last governess. Eight years later Beatrix expanded it into a book, printed at her own expense because six publishers had rejected it. Longer by one-third than the original letter, it had forty-two line illustrations taken from pen-and-ink drawings; only the frontispiece was coloured.

Success and a second private edition galvanized Frederick Warne into publishing the familiar version in 1902, for which Beatrix had to make a new set of illustrations in watercolour. Ever the practical artist, she solved the problem of 'rather uninteresting colour' (the subjects were 'most of them rabbit brown and green') by relieving them with Peter's blue jacket and touches of red, in the robin.

◁ **'Mr. McGregor ... ran after Peter, waving a rake'**
***[1901]***

An interesting and unconventional composition, but it was left out of the privately printed edition. Mr. McGregor is invisible except for one hand holding a rake; a similar device is used in the rabbit pie picture (*see page* 103).

*Pen-and-ink and pencil, with a little white paint*
*image 80x105mm on sheet 118x180mm*
NT

◁ **'She grew herbs and rabbit tobacco'**
***[1901]***

Several of the original pictures, and three pages on the home life of Mrs. Rabbit, were eliminated from Warne's full-colour trade edition, but some text was moved to *The Tale of Benjamin Bunny* (1904).

Mrs. Rabbit's lop ears are expressive: Peter is not pulling his weight.

*Pen-and-ink*
*image 87x75mm on sheet 117x177mm*
NT

▽ **'One table-spoonful to be taken at bed-time'**
*[1901]*
Better drawn than the coloured frontispiece, but omitted from Warne's edition. The image is reversed, and more of Peter is visible than in the final version of this scene (page 60).
*Pen-and-ink*
*image 85x80mm on sheet 107x156mm*
NT

◁ **'His mother put him to bed, and made some camomile tea'**
*[1907]*
Parody of a 'genre' scene, but set in a burrow. It was redrawn in close-up for the ninth printing (September 1907) (*see right*), when the worn colour blocks had to be re-engraved. Surprisingly, this more accomplished 'duplicate' was replaced in about 1911 by the original, weaker version (*see below*).
*Watercolour and pen-and-ink over pencil, pencil frame*
*image (vignetted) 101x84mm, frame 91x85mm, on sheet 145x102mm*
V&A (Linder Bequest)

▷ *The Tale of Peter Rabbit* (page 81)
*[1907-1911]*
PC

▽ *The Tale of Peter Rabbit* (page 66)
*1902 and current edition*

## The Tailor of Gloucester

**Two designs for the privately printed edition of *The Tailor of Gloucester* *[1902-1903]***

*The Tailor* was Beatrix Potter's 'own favourite' amongst her little books.

**◁ Rats dancing the heys in the Mayor's cellar**
The carousing rats were expelled, perhaps because they made drunkenness seem so attractive. Potter expressively punctuates her note in the original manuscript: 'not included in the later editions!!?'

**▽ Mice embroidering the Mayor's coat**
This mouse picture was redrawn for Warne's trade edition (page 42).
*Watercolour and pen-and-ink, pen-and-ink frames images 100x84mm (rats) and 83x100mm (mice) on sheet 105x185mm*
V&A (Linder Bequest)

▷ China and mice on the dresser, from *The Tailor of Gloucester* (page 26)
*1903*
Fine ceramics lovingly recorded, but they were shown to better advantage in the unorthodox composition of an unused alternative picture, based on the design from the privately printed edition. For publication the figures had to be more dominant: the mice are larger, and the furnishings have been completely rearranged.

'The earlier books … were written for real children in picture letters of scribbled pen and ink …'

25 November 1940, to Bertha Mahony Miller

## The Tale of Two Bad Mice

◁ **Hunca Munca chops at the plaster ham: unused design for *The Tale of Two Bad Mice* *[1904]***
A rough sketch with great vitality in the body language, and in the expressive ears.
*Watercolour over pencil, pencil frame image (vignetted) 133x122mm on sheet 162x159mm*
NT

▷ **'It's as hard as the hams at the cheese-monger's', from *The Tale of Two Bad Mice* (page 22)**
***1904***
Missing from the book picture are the rumpled tablecloth, and the blowsy pink wallpaper flowers which emphasize doll's house scale: a perfect setting for mice.

'… I confess that afterwards I painted most of the little pictures mainly to please myself. The more spontaneous the pleasure – the more happy the result.'

**25 November 1940, to Bertha Mahony Miller**

# The Tale of Mrs. Tiggy-Winkle

◁ **Mrs. Tiggy-Winkle: unfinished variant for the cover picture of *The Tale of Mrs. Tiggy-Winkle***
***[1905]***
Kitty Macdonald, the washerwoman at Dalguise, was the original inspiration for this much-loved hedgehog. Mrs. Tiggy-Winkle is dressed as a working woman of the period, with tucked up print frock and striped petticoat, but there the likeness ends: the eye betrays her essential wildness.

Beatrix used a cottonwool dummy for drawing the clothes; it terrified her rabbit. For the figure she used her pet hedgehog. 'If she is propped up on end for half an hour, she first begins to yawn pathetically, and then she *does* bite!'
*Watercolour and pen-and-ink over pencil*
*image 127x124mm on sheet 211x179mm*
V&A (Linder Bequest)

◁ **Mrs. Tiggy-Winkle at her washtub: preliminary sketch for the title page**
***[1905]***
Given by Leslie Linder in 1971 to Sir Frederick Ashton, dancer and choreographer, as a memento of their collaboration on the film of the Royal Ballet's *Tales of Beatrix Potter*, in which Ashton danced the role of Mrs. Tiggy-Winkle.
*Pencil*
*image 75x80mm on sheet 75x150mm*
PC

## The Tale of Tom Kitten

▽ **'Tom Kitten was very fat, and he had grown …', from *The Tale of Tom Kitten* (page 18)**
***[1907]***
Tom Kitten as anti-hero, with bursting buttons and an expression of dumb insolence. He reminds one of the insubordinate Peter: Beatrix found rebellious characters more interesting. Dressed, for the moment, in 'elegant and uncomfortable clothes' and even trousers, Tom loses nothing of his feline qualities or his personality.
*Watercolour and pen-and-ink over erased pencil, pencil frame added by printer*
*image (vignetted) 97x88mm on sheet 112x105mm*
NT

## The Tale of Mr. Jeremy Fisher

◁△▷ **Three unfinished preliminary drawings for *The Tale of Mr. Jeremy Fisher* *[1906?]***
All three designs, formerly mounted together and given to Stephanie Hyde Parker, a young cousin, have faint pencil frames as a guide for eventual vignettes (frontispiece, pages 30 and 56). One picture is inscribed: 'grasshopper', 'tortoise', 'newt'; beneath is a pencil study of a grasshopper.

Uncharacteristically, in the picture of Jeremy on his lily-leaf punt (*above*), Beatrix has completed the head before the background.
*Pen-and-ink and pencil; watercolour and pen-and-ink over pencil, with corrections in white paint; pen-and-ink and pencil*
*lh image 116x97mm on sheet 204x127mm; centre image (vignetted) 99x97mm on sheet 203x128mm; rh images 110x98mm and 11x31mm on sheet 191x131mm (all unevenly trimmed)*
V&A (Linder Bequest)

▷ Jeremy hops home, from *The Tale of Mr. Jeremy Fisher* (page 49)
*[1906]*
The vegetation is recorded from frog's-eye view: in the foreground are water forget-me-nots and a tussock of cowslips and grass straight out of the fungus studies. Beyond, tall foxgloves shelter Jeremy's tiny house.
*Watercolour and pen-and-ink over erased pencil image (vignetted) 111x97 on sheet 127x108mm*
NT

## The Tale of Jemima Puddle-Duck

◁ **'Jemima Puddle-Duck was not much in the habit of flying', from *The Tale of Jemima Puddle-Duck* (page 17)**
***1908***
Flapping her shawl to gain height, 'she flew beautifully when she had got a good start'. The next picture, in which she skims over the tree-tops, is given 'a sense of height and movement over a landscape too large to paint' (Josefina de Vasconcellos, 2004). *The Tale of Jemima Puddle-Duck* contains some of the artist's most idyllic vistas.
*Watercolour and pen-and-ink over erased pencil image (vignetted) 112x96mm on sheet 127x106mm*
NT

◁ **Jemima Puddle-Duck: sketch for the title page of *Jemima Puddle-Duck's Painting Book***
***[1925]***
Apart from some foxglove studies for the original Tale, this is one of a very few surviving preliminary drawings of Jemima herself. Its subtlety and life are lost in the coarse black outlines of the printed painting book, for which Beatrix thoughtfully commissioned additional separate sheets so that children could display their work.
*Pencil*
*160x103mm on sheet 240x175mm*
PC

△ Illustration after Otto Speckter, from *Hanne Nüte un de lütte Pudel*. Wismar: Hinstorff, 2nd edition
*1875*
A wood engraving from a *Plattdeutsch* folk tale by Fritz Reuter, first published in 1865: surely an ancestress of the 'vain and foolish bird', although a bonneted duck on the wing in Rupert Potter's sketchbook may also have fuelled the artist's imagination.
PC

# The rhyme books

**Intrigued by dialect and folklore,** and wishing to emulate the nursery rhyme picture books of Randolph Caldecott, Beatrix Potter planned a book of rhymes 'in a style between Caldecott's and the Baby's Opera (by Walter Crane)'; she could at least 'try to do better than Peter Rabbit'. After the death of Norman Warne, her fiancé, it was put on one side.

Several illustrations for individual rhymes had already been finished in colour in the 1890s. A few were made into little keepsake gift booklets (1896–1897) or even prepared for publication (*see* 'The Three Little Mice', *pages 92–3*). By 1902 Potter was considering the animal rhymes which Caldecott had left out, and sketching more illustrations. Her manuscript dummy for the '1905 Book of Rhymes' was conceived in generous size and ornate style. It contains rough pictorial layouts, many with decorative borders enclosing the text; ideas came from studying illuminated manuscripts at the Victoria and Albert Museum. Out of the thirty original rhymes she sent to Norman Warne (a few are limericks in the manner of Lear), five were eventually included in *Appley Dapply's Nursery Rhymes*. A number of the designs were never published (*see also* 'The Toads' Tea Party', *page 54*). Some were reworked for publication in 1917, and others in 1922 for the mainly traditional *Cecily Parsley's Nursery Rhymes*, Beatrix Potter's last book in the 'Peter Rabbit' format.

## 'I have thought of ever so many more rhymes – most extremely odd ones some of them!'

**20 October 1904, to Norman Warne**

## Appley Dapply's Nursery Rhymes and the unpublished 'Book of Rhymes'

△ **'Come dance a jig, to my Granny's pig', from the original block**
*[ca. 1900?]*
The setting of this design, perhaps intended for a greetings card, combines features of two holiday houses in Hertfordshire: Bedwell Lodge and Bush Hall. Caldecottian in style, it was at last printed in brown ink, as originally intended, by Battledore Ltd. of Kingston, New York in 1995. Potter made two illustrations for this rhyme, but neither was ever published, nor was the rhyme included in her 1905 manuscript dummy. She apparently sent it to her Drawing Society for comment: 'Nobody cares for the cocks & hens; & it comes rather near Caldecott's cat & fiddle, & comparisons are undesirable.' (28 July 1902)
*Proof printed in brown ink*
*image 90x115mm on sheet ca. 170x230mm*
PC

**'Appley Dapply': a rhyme in three scenes**
***[1891]***

A trio of designs was apparently prepared for publication as greetings cards or, more plausibly, as a booklet. A little picture of jam tarts on a plate, captioned 'Who Stole the Tarts?', apparently belongs to the same set. The original Scenes 1 and 3, both dated 1891, were reworked for *Appley Dapply's Nursery Rhymes* (1917); the mice become squatter and darker, and Scene 3 is reversed. A new drawing had to be made for Scene 2, the original having been mislaid. Potter refers to these illustrations as the earliest of all.

**◁ 'Appley Dapply, a little brown mouse, Goes to the cupboard in somebody's house'**

The panelled walls, as in the 'White Rabbit' designs, are reminiscent of Bedwell Lodge.
*Watercolour over pencil, pencil frame*
*image 91x114mm on sheet 124x153mm*
NT

**◁ 'In somebody's cupboard there's everything nice ...'**

The original finished watercolour for Scene 2, missing when *Appley Dapply's Nursery Rhymes* was being compiled for publication. In the 1930s it was found again and given to a child friend; in 1987 its owner, now elderly, heard of the Beatrix Potter exhibition at the Tate Gallery and offered it for public display.

The mouse turns her back to the viewer, her tail curves over the floor, and the tarts are still on the shelf. 'Everything nice', in Potter's view, includes bottles of home-made wine.
*Watercolour over pencil, pencil frame*
*image 90x115mm*
PC

▷ **'In somebody's cupboard ...': the replacement design**
*[1917?]*
Adapted from an early sketch for Scene I, and specially drawn for the 1917 rhyme book. Potter's style has naturally altered over the years. Her colours are brighter but the drawing is less careful, and seems rushed; the panelling is only roughly indicated. Appley Dapply now looks out at the viewer, and holds her tail high.
*Watercolour and pen-and-ink over pencil, pen-and-ink frame*
*image 91x114mm on sheet 124x164mm*
NT

▷ **'Appley Dapply has little sharp eyes,**
**And Appley Dapply is *so* fond of pies!'**
The sense of movement is enhanced by the horizontal lines of the panelling and Appley Dapply's extended tail.
*Watercolour over pencil, pencil frame*
*image 90x115mm on sheet 123x144mm*
NT

◁ **'There was an old woman who lived in a shoe'**
*[1905?]*
Beatrix made a booklet of this 'ancient rhyme' as a Christmas gift for her cousin Caroline Hutton. It is the only traditional rhyme included in *Appley Dapply* (pages 20ff); a peacefully knitting mouse illustrates the second verse.

This drawing is different in both colour and detail from the published version. Beatrix removed it from the manuscript 'Book of Rhymes', now in the National Trust collection, to preserve in a portfolio.
*Watercolour and sepia ink over pencil, with touches of white paint, pencil frame, bottom corners of text roughly indicated*
*image 94x122mm, frame 159x122mm, on sheet 211x179mm*
V&A (Linder Bequest)

▷ **Daffodils in a jug**
*[ca. 1900?]*
A similar jug sustains Old Mister Prickly Pin.

The Drawing Society thought it 'very pretty & very well painted', approving of the indistinct background, which echoes the swirling colours of the glaze.
*Watercolour over pencil, with highlights in white oil paint, pencil frame*
*image as sheet 194x170mm*
V&A (Linder Bequest)

◁ **'Old Mister Prickly Pin'**
*[ca. 1902]*
A portrait of Mrs. Tiggy-Winkle's uncle, for the unpublished Book of Rhymes. In *Appley Dapply's Nursery Rhymes* (page 19), redrawn and renamed 'Old Mr. Pricklepin', he is an altogether more farouche creature.

'I considered the hedgehog was about the best drawing I ever made', Beatrix Potter wrote in 1920.
*Watercolour and pen-and-ink over pencil, on thin board*
*image (vignetted) 132x165mm, including wash background 154x195mm, on sheet 160x201mm*
V&A (Linder Bequest)

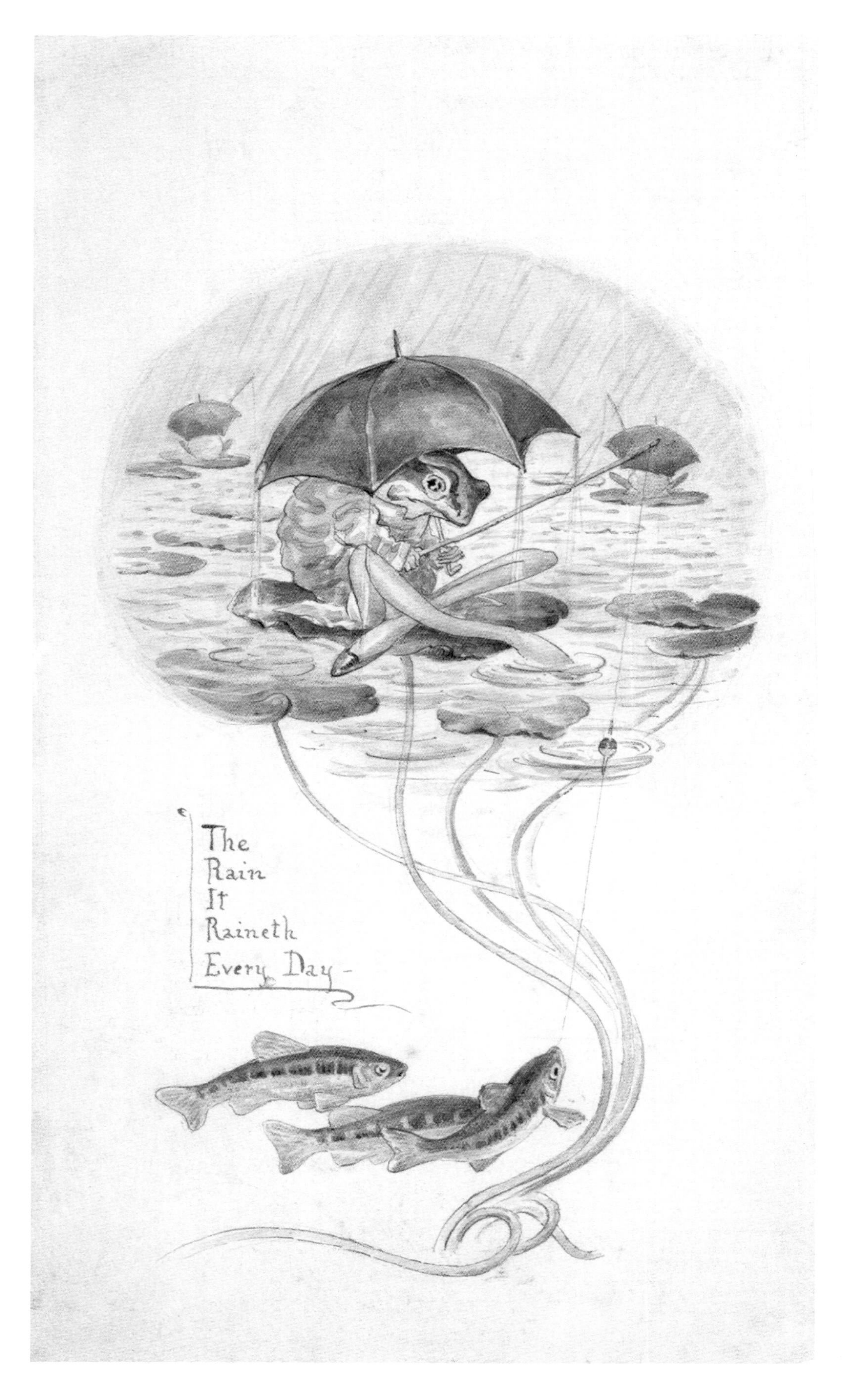


◁ **'The rain it raineth every day': frog fishing** ***[1898-1900]***

The title is from Shakespeare, but the design accompanies an unpublished rhyme, 'Fishes come bite!', and anticipates the frontispiece of *The Tale of Mr. Jeremy Fisher*. Two companion drawings in similar style, each dated 1898 and depicting a snail with its young, illustrate an 'extra' rhyme, 'There was an old snail with a nest'. Their current whereabouts is unknown.

A receding perspective of cross-legged frogs on lily-pads links foreground and background as in 'Dicky's Cake Dance', an exuberant but less sophisticated picture of the same period (*see page 84*).

The whiplash line, reminiscent of plant forms in Art Nouveau ornament, looks forward to the arabesques of Potter's endpaper designs in her 'little books'.

*Watercolour and pen-and-ink over erased pencil image 138x87mm on sheet 179x113mm*

V&A (Linder Bequest)

## Cecily Parsley's Nursery Rhymes

▷ **'Gentlemen came every day': frontispiece design for *Cecily Parsley's Nursery Rhymes* (1922) *[1917-1922]***

A favourite rhyme subject, which Potter illustrated more than any other except the knitting mouse. Quoted in a fragment of code writing, its earliest appearance is in a Christmas keepsake booklet. In 1902 Beatrix presented a larger version, with exceptionally relaxed and convivial rabbits, to her young friend Noël Moore for his album.

Originally intended for the 1905 'Book of Rhymes', this design, redrawn, was eventually published in *Cecily Parsley's Nursery Rhymes*. The rabbit customers have turned into sober citizens, and one has exchanged his pipe for a newspaper.

*Watercolour and pen-and-ink over pencil, pen-and-ink frame*
*image 156x180mm on sheet 169x190mm*
NT

▷ **Old Mr Bunny: an unused design *[ca. 1893?]***

A décor with rabbit-motif tiles, modification of the setting for 'Gentlemen came every day'. The 'little old buck-rabbit enjoying a pipe of rabbit-tobacco' appears in the privately printed *Peter Rabbit* (1901) and again, with altered text, in *The Tale of Benjamin Bunny*.

In 1892 the foreman at a frame shop had taught Beatrix how to draw 'a correct oval' as for this vignette, 'very ingenious and useful'.

*Watercolour and some pen-and-ink over pencil, on thin paper*
*image (vignetted) 104x72mm on sheet 165x114mm*
NT

△ **Cecily Parsley brewing cider**

*[1905?]*

The down-house, or farm kitchen, at Hill Top. Cecily Parsley, who 'brewed good ale', tips apples into a pancheon, among kegs and bottles, and herbs hung up to dry. Usually so accurate in her depiction of technical detail, Potter has misplaced the spigot, for the sake of the composition.

*Watercolour, bodycolour and pen-and-ink, on thin card*

*image 157x182mm on sheet 191x225mm*

LT

△ 'Cecily Parsley lived in a pen', redrawn for *Cecily Parsley's Nursery Rhymes* (page 6) *[1917-1922]*

The rabbit's head has been rather clumsily redrawn, as if superimposed on the background. At the publisher's insistence, the apples were changed to cowslips and the barrels of cider to cowslip wine – but cider apples are still in evidence, merely transferred from bowl to shelf!

*Watercolour and pen-and-ink over pencil, with touches of white paint, black ink frame*
*image 158x182mm on sheet 171x196mm*

NT

△ **'I can't find my way home!', from *Cecily Parsley's Nursery Rhymes* (page 19)**
***[1902?]***
'I had better have this back, to alter shape; it is a *much* better picture than P Bland.'

The only known complete set of designs for 'This little pig' was done in 1897 for a 'niece cousin', Stephanie Hyde Parker of Melford Hall; the signpost is lettered 'To Melford'. For this version the lettering has been changed and the image reversed. Foliage in the foreground is drawn in the same pen and wash technique as the 1903 garden backgrounds for *Benjamin Bunny*.
*Watercolour and pen-and-ink over pencil, pencil partial frame*
*image 207x279mm on sheet 228x279mm*
NT

▽ **'Ninny Nanny Netticoat'**

*[ca. 1902?]*

One of several variant designs for this candle riddle, related to the rhyme 'Little Nancy Etticoat'. It was redrawn smaller for *Cecily Parsley's Nursery Rhymes,* with red-gold tints and without the mousehole, identical to one in an earlier 'toy picture'.

*Watercolour and pen-and-ink over pencil image 153x205mm on sheet 157x210mm (unevenly trimmed)*

LT

# Sawrey books

## ‘It is as nearly perfect a little place as I ever lived in.’

***Journal* 17 November 1896**

Beatrix Potter was introduced to the village of Sawrey in 1896 and subsequently made her home there. *The Pie and the Patty-Pan* was the first of her books with a Sawrey setting; a succession of tales celebrating Sawrey followed, including *Samuel Whiskers, Ginger and Pickles, Pigling Bland* and, many years later, *The Fairy Caravan.*

◁ **'She was too early, and she had to wait a little': unused design for *The Pie and the Patty-Pan***
***[1902]***
Duchess walks decorously on her hind legs, carrying her 'tussie-mussie'; in the book she bounds along, posy in mouth. On the back is an inscription by W. A. Herring, Production Manager of Frederick Warne, indicating that this design had been considered for the book.
*Sepia ink or paint over pencil*
*image (vignetted) 165x225mm on sheet 210x285mm*
BPS

▽ **Ribby on the stairs: unused design for *The Pie and the Patty-Pan***
***[1902]***
A Sawrey interior at one of the three Lakefield Cottages, with geraniums on the window ledge and a sunbonnet on the wall. Potter usually completed her backgrounds first, before filling in the roughly sketched figures.

After producing several 'little' books, she felt the need for more space to do justice to the rich detail of her drawings. For the first version of *The Pie and the Patty-Pan* she accordingly made more than twenty studies in a generous size and sepia line. Norman Warne had hoped to reproduce them in brown ink, but only a few of these early designs were used, much adapted and printed in black.
*Sepia ink or paint over pencil, faint pencil frame*
*image 191x199mm, frame 188x222mm, on sheet 194x246mm*
V&A (Linder Bequest)

◁ **'Chippendale' and Queen Anne chairs at Fawe Park, Derwentwater**
***1903***
'If ever I had a house I would have old furniture, oak in the dining room, and Chippendale in the drawing room.' (*Journal*, 10 June 1884) Beatrix Potter relished fine craftsmanship, and was ahead of the times in her enjoyment of Chippendale chairs and old oak.

After her marriage, furniture collecting became a mission. She wrote informed notes on carved oak, then considered old-fashioned, and secured at the sale-rooms good pieces for her Lake District properties. Much of the furniture found its way into book illustrations; a chair in this drawing appears in *The Tale of Samuel Whiskers*.
*Sepia ink or paint over pencil*
*images 257x207mm on sheet 269x209mm*
V&A (Linder Bequest)

▷ **'Moppet and Mittens have grown up into very good rat-catchers', from *The Tale of Samuel Whiskers* (page 73)**
***[1908]***
One of the largest illustrations in the book, and a picture in its own right. Unusually, the figures do not dominate, but are part of a larger scene: Sawrey with spring blossom, ferns and a compost heap.
*Watercolour and sepia ink or paint over pencil, sepia frame*
*image 159x127mm on sheet 174x141mm*
NT

◁ **View from the roof of Hill Top Farm: a background for *The Tale of Samuel Whiskers* *[1908?]***

This picture, which Potter liked, was put in to counteract the effect of 'a string of sooty inside pictures'. In the preliminary version, but not in the published book, lightly sketched birds are observed by a white kitten.

*Watercolour and sepia ink or paint over pencil, sepia frame*

*image 159x125mm*

PC

▽ **'The chimney stack stood up above the roof like a little stone tower', from *The Tale of Samuel Whiskers* (page 34)**

***1908***

Artistic licence has improved the composition, adding distance and height to the hills beyond.

*Reproduction of original book picture (watercolour and sepia ink or paint)*

*image 113x91mm*

PC

# Book design

▷ **Decorative endpaper: design no. 1**
*[1903]*
Title page and cover should be strong and clear, but an endpaper 'ought to be something to rest the eye between the cover and the contents of the book; like a plain mount for a framed drawing.'

The Tales were issued at first with plain endpapers; the familiar coloured endpaper was first used in August 1903, for *Squirrel Nutkin*, *The Tailor of Gloucester*, and the fifth printing of *Peter Rabbit*. Potter devised nine designs; normally a pair was used in each book, and new animal characters were introduced as they appeared. Delicate colours, used at first to avoid heaviness in such small books, were intensified in later printings, and for the foreign editions all lettering was removed.
*Watercolour and pen-and-ink over erased pencil image 157x123mm on sheet 203x162mm*
NT

As the illustrator of her own books, with an exceptional flair for layout and graphic design, Beatrix Potter was involved at every stage of production. She worked up her ideas in dummies, writing out the stories in cheap exercise books and sketching the illustrations on separate slips of paper pasted opposite each brief page of text. Her designs were usually reduced by one-third to one-quarter for reproduction.

Vignetted pictures in colour mixed most happily with the text. Line illustrations, framed only in *Mr. Tod*, were more successful in other books as free shapes, but she considered that illustrations with edges needed borders: 'the black frame pulls them together and sends back the distance.'

The placing of the pictures had to relate to the carefully allocated type block; punctuation or white space were cleverly used for dramatic effect. Potter took great pains with proof correction, ruthlessly commenting on colour balance and register. In the case of *Peter Rabbit*, however, the publisher's ideas prevailed. Her original cover layouts for Warne's *Peter Rabbit* (Peter running on all fours, an image from the privately printed edition), were ousted by the iconic image which she later dismissed as 'that idiotic prancing rabbit on the cover'.

◁ **Preliminary design for endpaper no. 1**
*[1903]*
Although the coloured version shows some improvements in arrangement and anatomy, this line drawing is livelier. The scrolled arabesques, more emphatic here, were printed in blue because a fine line could be achieved only by using a single colour: at that time a true black could not be achieved through the trichromatic process. Potter had experimented with scrolled layouts in her 'working copy' of the privately printed *Tailor of Gloucester*, but this final design is far more satisfying.

Endpaper 'no. I' was originally conceived in monochrome; the V&A collection has an intermediate drawing in sepia ink.
*Pen-and-ink over pencil; pencil*
*image 162x129mm on sheet 210x163mm*
NT

# 'I do so dislike that idiotic prancing rabbit on the cover!'

**23 February 1941, to Arthur Stephens**

▷▽ Narrative endpapers: designs 1 and 4 for *The Roly-Poly Pudding* (*The Tale of Samuel Whiskers*)
*[1908]*
An effective composition in which the solidity of the centrally placed sack contrasts with the volatility of the rats. Clothed, quasi-human individuals above contrast with scampering rats in a state of nature; the trio of dancers seems oblivious of the watching cat.
*Watercolour and sepia ink or paint over pencil images (vignetted) 126x127mm on sheet 141x138mm (no. 1), 117x113mm on sheet 135x135mm (no. 4)*
NT

◁▽ **Narrative endpapers: designs 1 and 2 for *Ginger and Pickles***
***[1909]***

Mouse and rat tails, infinitely adaptable, are invaluable components in any composition. Potter's handling of bottle, box and twine harks back to her schoolroom exercises in still life.

Narrative endpapers suited the larger format of *The Roly-Poly Pudding* and *Ginger and Pickles*; they were succeeded by designs which more blatantly advertised the books.

*Watercolour and pen-and-ink over pencil images (vignetted) 90x87mm on sheet 133x123mm (no. 1), 88x89mm on sheet 135x129mm (no. 2)*

NT

▷ **Unfinished title page design for *The Roly-Poly Pudding* (*The Tale of Samuel Whiskers*) *[1908]***

Beatrix Potter drew title page layouts for *Peter Rabbit, Squirrel Nutkin,* and *The Tale of Two Bad Mice,* but this is her most elaborate of all. Arabesques, linked with rats' tails, echo the endpapers; the design was simplified for the published book, which first came out in a large format. In 1926, when the size was reduced and the title changed, this elegant layout disappeared as did the original frontispiece, again embellished with scrolled designs and dancing rats.

*Watercolour and pen-and-ink over pencil, corrections in white paint, pencil frame, pasted-on label*

*image 165x138mm, frame 185x140mm, on sheet 238x165mm*

NT

# LATER LIFE AND WORK

**Success brought Beatrix Potter financial independence,** and perhaps consoled her for the indifference of the academic establishment to her scientific research. In 1905 she bought her first Lake District property; in 1913 she married and moved to Castle Cottage, Sawrey. She kept Hill Top as a private place in which to write and draw, and as a working farm. No longer the dutiful daughter expected to run her parents' house in London, she found freedom, and a new life as wife, hill farmer, sheepbreeder and pioneering conservationist.

Soon after her marriage she became Secretary of a small and apparently short-lived art club, perhaps modelled on the Drawing Society to which she had subscribed fifteen years before. 'I cannot paint quite so delicately as I did twenty-five years ago; but I can still draw.' She sketched and 'scribbled', but mainly for recreation: 'somehow when one is up to the eyes in work with real animals it makes one despise paper-book-animals.' Hours at the microscope long ago had strained her eyes; evenings at Hill Top painting by candlelight made it difficult to see 'clean colours'. In exasperation she wrote to Warne, 'You don't suppose I shall be able to continue these d. . . .d little books when I am dead and buried!!'

Still interested in art and literature, she delighted in discovering new writers and illustrators: A. A. Milne, Arthur Ransome, and Dr. Seuss. Her critical faculties were as sharp as ever; she wrote not long before her death in 1943: 'I hope I am able to appreciate "style" . . . but need style involve downright out-of-drawing?' Disney's proposal to film *Peter Rabbit* was simply unacceptable; no doubt she would have disapproved of present-day omnibus editions and cartoon vulgarizations.

Generous with advice and encouragement to young friends who tried to write or paint, she was equally generous with her work, giving away drawings, and providing designs for charity greetings cards. She wished all her paintings to be 'given to some public collection, not sold'.

# Farming and domestic life

▷ **Kep** ***1907***
'Strongly muscled and lightly boned', Kep was Beatrix Potter's first and favourite collie, immortalized in *The Tale of Jemima Puddle-Duck*. Beatrix has left thumb and finger prints on her original clay figure, which she incised with the date.

There are references to a 'clay Peter', and a plaster model of a butchered pig, but the only other examples of modelling known to survive are some early plaques. This facsimile was made in the late 1980s by the Cumbrian sculptor Clive Barnard.
*'Resin-bronze' replica of clay figure, on wooden plinth*
*figure 148x47x113mm high*
PC

▷ **Studies of Scotch Fly**
*1 June 1929*
Beatrix Potter respected and admired dogs, sheep and horses, but found them difficult to draw. Scotch Fly at three years old was 'an extremely good sheep dog, only very nervous'.
*Pencil*
*images 199x155mm on visible sheet 210x167mm*
WA

◁ **Beatrix with Kep**
*[May 1913]*
Taken four months before her marriage by an American visitor, Charles G. Y. King. Beatrix wears her familiar coat and skirt in Herdwick tweed.
*Photograph: gelatin silver bromide print*
*200x146mm*
V&A (Linder Bequest)

## 'Somehow when one is up to the eyes in work with real animals it makes one despise paper-book-animals …'

**6 May 1918, to Fruing Warne**

△ **Portrait of a sheep**

*[ca. 1910?]*

Executed in a daringly experimental style and a vivid palette: bright red, cobalt, ochre, black, sage-green, browns and greys, and a little white.

*Watercolour over pencil*

*image 118x179mm on sheet 227x191mm*

V&A (Linder Bequest)

▷ **Six Herdwick rams**

*[ca. 1910?]*

As Mrs. Heelis, Beatrix Potter became a hill farmer and renowned breeder of the hardy Herdwick sheep. Her flocks of breeding ewes were left to the National Trust as part of the Heelis Bequest.

*Pencil*

*image 163x114mm on sheet 177x114mm*

LT

△ **Beatrix Potter and William Heelis at Bolton Gardens**

***14 October 1913***

Taken by Rupert Potter on the day before their wedding: the least well-known, and happiest, of four poses. In one Beatrix stands, in another she sits; in a third both are standing, but here their hands are close and companionable. Her marriage, wrote her cousin Caroline Hutton in 1944 to the recently widowed William, was 'a very great happiness'.

*Photoprint (original 119x165mm)*

Cotsen

△ **Hill Top porch at night**
***15 December 1912***
A welcoming light streams from the doorway. This little drawing was done as a Christmas card for a member of the Heelis family, but may never have been sent, although Beatrix has added the address 'Hill Top Farm'. A larger version of the same scene is in the Linder Bequest.

As Mrs. Heelis, Beatrix lived nearby at Castle Farm but still kept her first Sawrey home. 'It is here I go to be quiet and still with myself.'
*Watercolour over pencil*
*image 93x62mm on sheet 114x178mm (114x89mm folded)*
PC

▷ **'And they drink bucketfuls of milk': unused variant for *The Tale of Pigling Bland* (page 14)**
***[1913]***
Most artists of the time saw no point in showing the disagreeable side of country life. Aunt Pettitoes smiles, and so does the tranquil landscape; in the background is Hill Top Farm. Fond as she was of her pigs and sheep, Potter took a realistic view. 'It does not do to be sentimental on a farm, I am going to have some lambskin hearthrugs.'
*Watercolour and sepia ink over pencil, black ink frame*
*image 159x128mm on sheet 196x166mm*
V&A (Linder Bequest)

◁ **'Quite a speckled pig': unused drawing for *The Tale of Pigling Bland***
***[1912-1913]***
'I think I shall put *myself* in the next book.' A measled Chin-chin is attended by Aunt Goosey (Aunt Pettitoes) and Beatrix Potter. Glimpsed as a tiny figure at the end of *The Roly-Poly Pudding*, Beatrix plays a more active, but featureless, part in *The Tale of Pigling Bland*. This scene takes place in an early manuscript version with the title 'Eight Little Pigs'.

The thick black ink line, that she so disliked, is evidence that this drawing was actually prepared for the printer.
*Black ink over pencil, with corrections in white paint, on thin paper*
*image 85x124mm on sheet 132x208mm*
NT

◁ **'Pigling Bland, who was a sedate little pig, looked solemnly at his mother', from *The Tale of Pigling Bland* (page 19)**
***1913***
In the last book to be published before her marriage Beatrix Potter celebrates her Hill Top pigs, and Kep. An alternative design includes a more complete self-portrait and shows more of Kep, but this was the picture selected for publication. Beatrix appears again in a line drawing (page 21), bending over the 'hopelessly volatile' and inattentive Alexander.

Sawrey
nr Ambleside
Jan 22.24

Dear Mr Warne,

I enclose copy of letter which I am posting to the Editor of the Sunday Herald. I don't suppose the Herald circulates amongst the class who purchase my books, but Sir J. Foster Fraser may repeat it elsewhere.

I have often read, and appreciated, articles by him in local papers. It is a very old mistake, although the Christian names are spelled differently. I usually take no notice, as even the insult of being mistaken for Mrs S Webb is preferable to publicity.

But if the Webbs are going to become prominent along with our new rulers, the error had better be contradicted; for I do not think that nice old fashioned people who like my books would like them quite so much if they believed them to be of socialist origin.

I wonder if people have thought that play was Mrs Webb's?! Has it been a success do you think? I noticed that the fourth week was advertised.

Mr Heelis is much edified by the portraits of Mr & Mrs Webb on the front page of the Herald; he says it is adding insult to injury to suggest that Miss Beatrix Potter is married 'to such a little animal'! He thinks it wants stopping.

I should not like my real name to have to come out; if

▷ **Self-caricature with pig, from a letter to Fruing Warne**

***22 January 1924***

Affronted that the *Sunday Herald* had taken her for the left-leaning Beatrice Webb (apparently forgetting that they were in fact distant cousins), Beatrix wishes to dispel the confusion. 'I think the best contradiction would be to get photographed along with a favourite pig or cow and get it inserted in some more genteel newspaper!'

She continues: 'I had lately a pig that continually stood on its hindlegs leaning over the pig stye, but it's hanging up, unphotographed & cured now.'

*Ink*

*image 28x95mm on sheet 230x177mm (second of 2 sheets)*

WA

the thing unfortunately spreads I think the best contradiction would be to get photographed along with a favourite pig or cow and get it inserted in some more genteel newspaper!

I had lately a pig that continually stood on its hindlegs leaning over the pig stye, but its hanging up, unphotographed & cured now.

Yrs truly
HB Heelis

Messrs F Warne & Co

What ever is Sir H Tripp driving at – he has some scheme that is going to bring in a deal of money but it never gets further than a mystery – his last letter had no stamps on it & cost 3d.

◁ **Sketches of the head of an old woman: Beatrix Potter's mother?**
*[ca. 1925?]*
Possibly the Potters' housemaid, but more likely to be Mrs. Potter herself. Beatrix rarely drew figures or faces, but in this near-caricature she forgets her inhibitions.
*Pencil*
*images 68x53mm on sheet 126x93mm*
V&A (Linder Bequest)

# The Fairy Caravan

△ **Cedar at Birds' Place, Camfield Place (headpiece to Chapter VII, page 51)**
Camfield Place in Hertfordshire was the house of Beatrix Potter's paternal grandparents, as magical a lost domain as Dalguise House in Perthshire.
*Pen-and-ink, with corrections in white paint*
*image 54x102mm*
WA

***The Fairy Caravan* was first published** by David McKay of Philadelphia in 1929, but not until 1952 by Warne. Beatrix felt it 'too personal' to publish in her own country, and too local to the Lake District for the general public. 'I am sure the average Londoner would care nothing about Herdwick sheep! That chapter [in which she honours the ancient Herdwick lineage] made my old shepherd cry with pleasure; that is appreciation worth having.'

'In the middle of the mossy grass plot stood the glory of the garden – the cedar.'

*The Fairy Caravan* Chapter VII

◁ **Mary Ellen, the farm cat, stares at the fire (page 142)**

A favourite drawing of Beatrix Potter's elderly cat Tamsine '(a seventeenth family arrived next day!)'. In this 'night scene by fire-glow and moonlight' (A. Parker, 1993) there is much vernacular detail, in copper, bellows and fire-crane.

*The Fairy Caravan* has only six colour plates, undistinguished in comparison with the many line illustrations. Commentators have too often neglected Beatrix Potter's mastery of draughtsmanship.

*Pen-and-ink*

*image 162x119mm*

WA

▷ **Pony Billy crossing the ford, from *The Fairy Caravan* (headpiece to Chapter XVII, page 127)**
The swirling ripples of this nocturne recall the line technique of the illustrator Edmund Sullivan. Pony Billy was Beatrix Potter's own pony Dolly.
*Pen-and-ink, with some corrections in white paint*
*image 61x110mm*
WA

▽ **'Black shadows flung across the silver road ...' (headpiece to Chapter XVIII, page 137)**
'Dolly trotting over the shadows' near Ees Bridge, Sawrey. This 'haunted' moonlit vignette was one of Beatrix Potter's two favourite pictures in *The Fairy Caravan*.
*Pen-and-ink over erased pencil, with corrections in white paint*
*image 53x116mm*
WA

▽ **Craggy hillside with vixen and playing cubs (page 79)**

Potter copied the background for this illustration from one of her brother's landscape etchings. She understood the geological structure beneath her landscapes just as she understood the skeleton beneath the skin.

*Pen-and-ink, with corrections in white paint*

*image 131x121mm*

WA

△ **Craggy hillside at Newlands, near Keswick (or Broad How, Troutbeck); reproduction of an etching by Bertram Potter**
**1898**
Bertram Potter (1872–1918) became a talented etcher and painter of large landscapes in oils. He married a Scottish girl and lived at Ashyburn, near Hawick, as a gentleman farmer.
*Photoreproduction of an etching*
*image ca. 150x240mm*
PC

# Buildings, landscapes and gardens

◁ **'Coniston Old Hall, Lancashire – from nature'**
***1890***
Most of Beatrix Potter's chalk drawings date from 1884. She returned to the medium after a few years; her later studies include farm buildings, some at Bedwell Lodge, and bold duck heads done in white chalk on large sheets of brown paper. This example records a characteristic detail of Lake District vernacular architecture: a tall chimney with a circular shaft.
*Black chalk and pencil*
*image as sheet 291x228mm*
FLP

△ **'Harvest' by Esthwaite Water**
*[1902?]*
A painting circulated among members of the Drawing Society to which Beatrix Potter belonged at the end of the century while still living in London; her pen name was 'Bunny'. 'Rather a daring subject', one member comments on the back; the distance was generally praised, but the hurried foreground was considered to spoil the effect.
*Watercolour over pencil*
*image as sheet 254x353mm*
V&A (Linder Bequest)

◁ **'At Evening's Close': Eeswyke (formerly Lakefield), Sawrey**
***[1902?]***
The Potters stayed at this house overlooking Esthwaite Water in 1896 and 1902. Coniston Old Man is framed in the rose arch over the gate. 'An English Garden', seen from a different viewpoint, was painted a few years earlier in vivid blue-greens and mauves. Like 'Harvest', it was submitted to the Drawing Society.
*Watercolour, ink wash and sepia ink over pencil*
*image as sheet 293x227mm*
LT

▷ **Garden steps at Fawe Park, Derwentwater**
***31 July 1903***
One of 'every imaginable rabbit background, & miscellaneous sketches as well – about 70!' for *The Tale of Benjamin Bunny*, done in this terraced garden overlooking the lake. Potter called them 'scribbled', but many are finished paintings in their own right, used in the book with little alteration other than the addition of animal protagonists. On these steps Peter 'let the pocket-handkerchief go again' (page 37).
*Watercolour and black ink or paint over pencil*
*image as sheet 227x190mm*
FLP

## 'I never have cared tuppence … for popularity …'

**29 May 1919, to Fruing Warne**

◁ **Woodland with squirrels**

*[1903]*

Animals in their natural state and setting, probably in the Derwentwater woods near Lingholm, background for many of the *Squirrel Nutkin* pictures. A similar but altogether tidier glade frames the squirrel cavalcade on page 30. In the National Trust collection is a preliminary drawing of the squirrel and, in a sketchbook, the same scene without squirrels. The vignetted shape and treatment of foliage link this painting to rhyme illustrations such as 'The Toads' Tea Party' (*see page 54*).

*Watercolour and sepia ink or paint over pencil image (vignetted) 180x138mm on sheet 205x162mm*

V&A (Linder Bequest)

▽ **View across Esthwaite Water**
***21 November 1909***
Esthwaite Water was Potter's favourite lake, which she drew at every season and in every mood. Bright tints capture sunlight on the fells and reflections on the water; wetted paper creates the effect of a damp atmosphere.
*Watercolour*
*image as sheet 178x254mm*
V&A (Linder Bequest)

△ **Clearing in a wood**
***16 November 1909***
'In copying nature it is possible to make the colour incorrect, but not to make it too solidly strong. Nature, with the exception of water and air, is made of colour.' (*Journal*, 7 March 1886)
*Watercolour (partly scraped off) over pencil*
*image as sheet 178x255mm*
FLP

◁ **Path through a wood**
***24 November 1909***
From a group of late *plein air* sketches in a fast impressionistic wash, done in the years before the First World War.
*Watercolour over pencil*
*image as sheet 178x129mm*
FLP

△ **Esthwaite Low Grounds**
***4 February 1911***
A quick sketch which summarizes an effect of light. Not immediately identifiable as a work by Beatrix Potter: she maintained that it is a pity for an artist to get into a groove, 'even a good groove'.
*Watercolour over pencil*
*image as sheet 139x228mm*
FLP

◁ **Hillside under snow with a stormy sky**
***11 January 1913***
Farming left little time for painting, except in winter and at night. After a heavy spring snow-fall in March 1909, Beatrix had spent five out of six consecutive days sketching in the fields and on the fells.
*Watercolour over pencil*
*image as sheet 254x178mm*
V&A (Linder Bequest)

▷ **Cart track under snow**
***[January 1913?]***
'Have you ever noticed what a peculiar blue the snow is during a white frost?' The transparent quality of watercolour perfectly achieves this effect.
*Watercolour over pencil*
*image as sheet 254x177mm*
V&A (Linder Bequest)

▷ **Cottage at Teignmouth**
*[1910?]*
An architectural peculiarity which caught the artist's eye. At this stage, except in her line illustrations for *The Fairy Caravan* and *Little Pig Robinson*, Potter's studies of buildings have become far less precise and free in style.
*Watercolour over pencil*
*image as sheet 228x141mm*
LT

◁ **Landscape without fox, by Esthwaite Water**
*[ca. 1910?]*
This landscape background was redrawn in brown ink, but printed in black, for the illustration of Mr. Tod on the lake-shore. The format is unusual: long horizontal lines give an impression of calm, soon to be disturbed by the ominous presence of a fox.
*Watercolour over pencil*
*image 105x207mm on sheet 123x209mm*
V&A (Linder Bequest)

◁ **Landscape with fox: preliminary study for *The Tale of Mr. Tod* (page 8)**
*[1912?]*
The novelty of *Mr. Tod* lies partly in its illustrations: only sixteen watercolours, and forty-two emphatically framed line drawings in woodcut style, reminiscent of the Eragny Press books illustrated by Lucien Pissarro.
*Sepia ink or paint over pencil, ink and pencil frame*
*image 84x199mm on sheet 133xca. 214mm*
FLP

△ **Teignmouth harbour from Salty Point, with fishing boats**
***[1910?]***
Painted in luminous wash over schematic underdrawing, and probably used as a background for the frontispiece of *The Tale of Little Pig Robinson*.
*Watercolour over pencil*
*image as sheet 140x228mm*
FLP

▽ **Beached boats on Salty Point, Teignmouth**
*[1910?]*
The strong solidity of the boats stands out against a flat middle distance.
*Watercolour over pencil*
*image as sheet 140x228mm*
V&A (Linder Bequest)

# The Tale of Little Pig Robinson

Pendennis Hotel
Falmouth
March 28. 94

My dear Eric

.. there are a great many ships here, some very large ones, there is one from Norway, and a French one unloading at the quay. Some of the sailors have little dogs, and cocks and hens on the ships. I have read about the owl & the pussy cat, who went to sea in a pea green boat, but I never saw anything of that kind till today.

I was looking at a ship called the Pearl of Falmouth which was being mended at the bottom because it had rubbed on a rock, when I heard something grunt!

◁ **Picture letter sent to Eric Moore from Falmouth**
***28 March 1894***
Little Pig Robinson first appears in this letter, but the idea for a harbour setting originated in a visit to Ilfracombe in April 1883. After some persuasion by her American publisher, David McKay Co., Potter finally agreed to prepare Pig Robinson's tale, her last 'little book', forty-seven years later.

Picture letter stories with 'pen-and-ink scribbles', borrowed back from young friends, served as the basis for her Tales. She made this 'file copy' from the original letter, now in the Cotsen Collection at Princeton University.
*Pen-and-ink over pencil (drawing); ink (text)*
*2 sheets 178x225, 179x228mm*
V&A (Linder Bequest)

**Line illustrations for *The Tale of Little Pig Robinson*. Philadelphia: David McKay Co. *1930***

Haymaking and weather interrupted work on the 'black and whites'. The American edition, which Potter preferred, has twenty-five more line illustrations, including head- and tailpieces, than the English version published by Frederick Warne in the same year.

▷ **The cat Susan meets the herring boats (tailpiece to Chapter I, page 18, and front endpaper)**

*Little Pig Robinson* is 'a comprehensive sample of our much-battered coasts': its backgrounds are an amalgam of Ilfracombe, Sidmouth, Lyme Regis and Teignmouth, and the net sheds of Hastings.

*Pen-and-ink*

*image 65x134mm on sheet 134x204mm*

FLP

▷ **Little Pig Robinson and 'the big dog Gypsy' (page 47)**

Another prominent chimney. Potter gave her original manuscript and twenty-nine drawings to the publisher's daughter, Margery McKay; the dog was drawn from a photograph of her Airedale.

*Pen-and-ink, with corrections in white paint, pencil frame*

*image 172x137 on sheet 205x163mm*

FLP

◁ **Little Pig Robinson looks into a shop window, in Lyme Regis (page 83)**
Beatrix Potter considered that this picture was 'the best black & white I ever did', but a few weeks earlier had written to Mr. McKay: 'I think myself that some of the chapter ends are the best drawings of any.'
*Pen-and-ink, with corrections in white paint, pencil frame*
*image 170x131mm on sheet 205x161mm*
FLP

## 'I cannot paint quite so delicately as I did twenty-five years ago; but I can still draw.'

**30 November 1927, to Mrs. Perry**

△ **Sim Ram's pony gig and his dog (tailpiece to Chapter V, page 89)**
'Don't you think black & whites look better top or bottom?'

Threatening storm clouds hang over the promontory.

*Pen-and-ink, with corrections in white paint, pencil frame*

*image 47x128mm on sheet 207x165mm*

FLP

▷ **The Owl and the Pussy Cat in their boat (for page 110)**
Intrigued since childhood by Edward Lear's ballad 'The Owl and the Pussy Cat', Beatrix Potter illustrated it in booklets and picture letters. This design, redrawn 'not so long' for a back endpaper, is a reflection rather than a copy of Lear, that other great artist of natural history – who caricatured his own serious work for fun.

*Pen-and-ink, with corrections in white paint, pencil frame*

*image 53x115 on sheet 205x163mm*

FLP

## Tributes

◁ **Wool shop with 'an old Sheep', from *Through the Looking-Glass, and what Alice found there*, by Lewis Carroll. London: Macmillan & Co.**

***1872***

When Beatrix Potter first encountered *Alice* at the age of six or seven, Tenniel's pictures immediately 'absorbed' her. She designed several illustrations for *Alice in Wonderland,* but this parody is her only known visual tribute to *Through the Looking Glass.*

PC

▷ **Fleecy Flock's wool shop, from *The Tale of Little Pig Robinson* (page 68)**

***1930***

A gesture is made to Tenniel's sheep in this portrait of Mrs. Flock, keeper of the wool shop. Not all Potter's late work in colour was unsuccessful, although by now she preferred to work in line.

*Watercolour and pen-and-ink over pencil, black ink frame*

*image 168x133mm on sheet 230x167mm*

NT

◁ ***Love Locked Out*, by Anna Lea Merritt *(1889)***

A painting which may have inspired the picture of a forlorn Peter.

*Reproduction by the Tate Gallery*

▽ ***In Disgrace*, by Charles Burton Barber**

The posture of the child model is very like that of Peter at the door. This portrait was exhibited at the Royal Academy's Summer Exhibition in 1886.

*Reproduction by Parnassus Gallery*

Beatrix Potter
Aug. 1927

▷ **Peter Rabbit locked out, redrawn for *The Horn Book Magazine***
***August 1927***

Surely a tongue-in-cheek parody of child portraits seen by Beatrix in her gallery-going youth. A more limited palette and a lack of precision in the line are evidence of late work, but the foliage is drawn in her style of the early 1900s. She signed herself 'Beatrix Potter', as was her custom when giving away drawings after her marriage.

In response to an urgent appeal by the National Trust to save 'a bit of our scenery' from development (Cockshott Point on Windermere), Beatrix sent to *The Horn Book Magazine* fifty drawings, copied and autographed, to be sold at a guinea each. Four were selected, but this one was rejected.

*Watercolour and sepia ink*
*image (vignetted) 94x74mm on sheet 203x134mm*
V&A (Linder Bequest)

◁ ***Sty Head Tarn, Borrowdale*, by John Constable**
***12 October 1806, Noon***
At the suggestion, and expense, of his uncle, Constable made a tour of the Lake District in early Autumn 1806. There he made many sketches, several of them in Borrowdale, where he revelled in clouds and stormy skies. One drawing is inscribed 'The finest scenery that ever was', but the solitude of the mountains 'oppressed his spirits'.
*Watercolour over pencil*
*image as sheet 121x269mm*
V&A (Paintings Collection)

▽◁ **Copy from a sketch by Constable of Sty Head Tarn, Borrowdale**
***[ca. 1900?]***
To Beatrix, the 'great, and *broad*-painting Constable' was one of the 'Immortals'. She copied this landscape at the South Kensington Museum, where she also studied mediaeval illuminated manuscripts and drew eighteenth-century costumes for *The Tailor of Gloucester*.
*Watercolour over pencil*
*image 117x252mm, overall size 129x252mm: rectangle with rh lower margin extended to form a label 12x100mm*
V&A (Linder Bequest)

△▷ **Illustration by Maurice Sendak, from *The Big Green Book*, by Robert Graves (Macmillan New York)**
***1962***
Sendak pays his respects to Potter in the detail of his pictures: a gate, a wall, a Bedwell Lodge interior, Hill Top, and the dormers and chimneys of Bush Hall.
PC

▷ **Bush Hall on the River Lea, Hertfordshire**
***15 August 1884***
One of a number of architectural studies dating from a holiday in summer 1884. Many years later Beatrix wrote on the back: 'These chalk drawings, in singularly good perspective, must have been done when I was 18.'
*Black chalk and charcoal, with some corrections in white paint*
*image 282x224mm on sheet 328x224mm (unevenly trimmed)*
LT

◁▽ ***The Tale of One Bad Rat*, by Bryan Talbot. Milwaukie, Oregon: Dark Horse Comics**
***1995***

A dark tale: the story of Helen Potter, an abused girl who escapes from London, comforted by Beatrix Potter's little books and the spirit of her pet rat. In this final part, she visits Hill Top where she discovers an unknown Potter work, 'The Tale of One Bad Rat'. The story ends in reconciliation and forgiveness. Symbolically, Helen learns to paint the Lakes from life, instead of copying from her heroine and namesake.

This award-winning graphic novel was selected as recommended reading by the *New York Times*. It is 'an ingenious, intertextual narrative that interweaves the charming, whimsical, and above all, the English vision of Beatrix Potter with a vision of England as it has become.' (A. Moore)

PC

# The 'little side shows'

PATENTS, DESIGNS, AND TRADE MARKS ACTS, 1883 to 1888.

Certificate of Registration of Design.

Rd. No. 423888

THE PATENT OFFICE: DESIGNS BRANCH,
25, SOUTHAMPTON BUILDINGS,
CHANCERY LANE, LONDON, W.C.,
1903.

This is to certify that the Design, of which annexed is a Copy, was registered this 28th day of December, 1903, in respect of the application of such Design to articles comprised in Class Twelve in pursuance and subject to the provisions of the Patents, Designs, and Trade Marks Acts, 1883 to 1888.

C. N. DALTON.

Messrs Fredk Warne & Co.

EXTRACT FROM DESIGNS RULES, 1893.

Rule 5.—For Rule 33 of the Designs Rules, 1890, shall be substituted the following Rule:—

33. Before delivery on sale of any article to which a registered design has been applied, the proprietor of such design shall if such article is included in Class 13 or Class 14 in the Third Schedule hereto cause each such article to be marked with the abbreviation Regd., and shall, if such article is included in any of the Classes 1 to 12 in the Third Schedule hereto, cause each such article to be marked with the abbreviation Rd., and also, in the case of articles other than lace, with the number appearing on the certificate of registration.

△ **The Peter Rabbit toy made by Beatrix Potter: Certificate of Registration of Design, assigned to F. Warne & Co.**
***28 December 1903***

'There is a run on toys copied from pictures. ... I am cutting out calico patterns of Peter.' Only a year after the publication of *The Tale of Peter Rabbit*, Potter made and promptly registered a Peter Rabbit doll, for Christmas 1903: 'the expression is going to be lovely; especially the whiskers – (pulled out of a brush!)' Always a good businesswoman, she was well aware of merchandising possibilities but anxious to keep strict control and maintain standards. Her original designs must be followed as faithfully as the medium allowed.

Beatrix Potter was one of the first artist-illustrators to start character licensing – nearly two decades before Disney. Other spin-offs soon appeared: a race game in 1919 (planned as early as 1904), a wallpaper frieze by 1905, painting books, music books, handkerchiefs in 1917, lantern slides and an excellently printed tea set by Grimwades Ltd in 1922, rubber toys by the Chorley Rubber Company in 1923, and charming tiles. Outstanding among the 'little side shows' are tiny bronze figurines by Fritz Bermann (1913), the 'Wiener Bronzen'.

*Gelatin silver bromide print*
*308x195mm (patent), 295x186mm (photograph)*
WA

◁ **Steiff 'Peter Rabbit' toy**
*[1904?]*
The pirated German doll, which Beatrix found '*very ugly*'. She registered a Jemima plush doll, but abandoned plans for her own Peter Rabbit doll and joined in the campaign for Tariff Reform against Liberal Free Trade. In January 1910 she wrote, 'my fingers are quite stiff with drawing posters.' Her design depicted a doll slumped against a tombstone, with the words 'Here lies the South London toy trade killed by free trade with Germany.'
*Grey velours, glass eyes, blue felt jacket, brass buttons, red felt shoes with leather soles*
*260x80x105mm*
WA

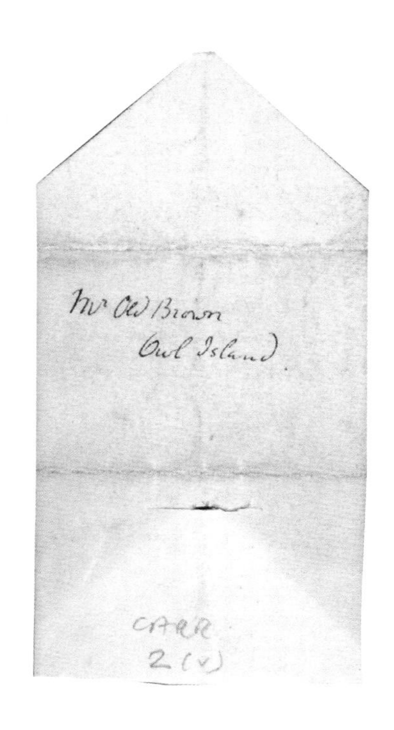
Mr Old Brown
Owl Island

CARR
2 (v)

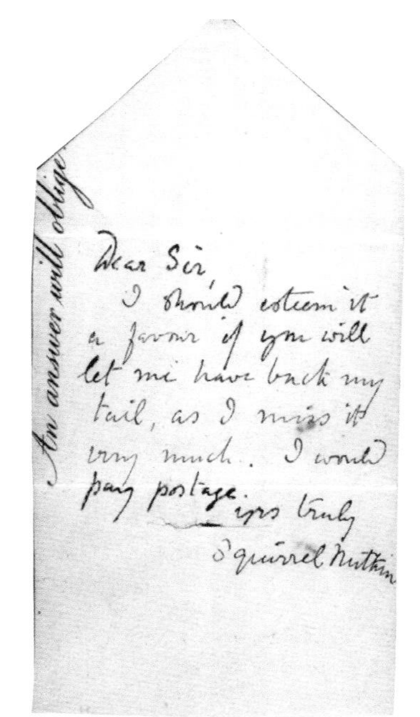
An answer will oblige

Dear Sir,
I should esteem it a favour if you will let me have back my tail, as I miss it very much. I would pay postage.
yrs truly
Squirrel Nutkin

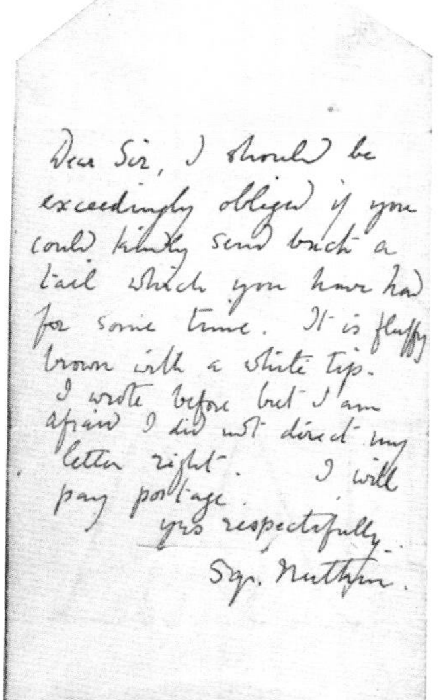
Dear Sir, I should be exceedingly obliged if you could kindly send back a tail which you have had for some time. It is fluffy brown with a white tip. I wrote before but I am afraid I did not direct my letter right. I will pay postage.
yrs respectfully
Sqr. Nutkin.

Dear Sir,
I write on behalf of my brother Nutkin to beg that as a great favour you would send him back his tail, for which he will gladly pay three bags of nuts. He never asks riddles now and he is truly sorry that he was so rude. Trusting that you continue to enjoy good health
I remain yrs obediently
Twinkleberry Squirrel.

△▷ **Miniature letters sent to Lucie and Kathleen Carr**
*[ca. 1905]*
From a group of twelve miniature letters presented to the V&A in 1996 by Miss Carr, the original 'Lucie' of *The Tale of Mrs. Tiggy-Winkle*. They tell of the continuing adventures of Potter's characters, as they corresponded with one another, and with her child friends. Squirrel Nutkin and his cousin implore Old Brown to return Nutkin's missing tail. The letters become progressively more formal, culminating in 'Rt Hon O. Brown Esq M.P.'; Old Brown at last replies, but in the third person, as to a social inferior.
*Ink*
*73x37mm, 90x45mm, 90x44mm, 90x45mm*
V&A (Carr Collection)

Mr Brown writes to say that he cannot reply to letters as he is asleep.
Mr Brown cannot return the tail.
He ate it some time ago; it nearly choked him.
Mr Brown requests Nutkin not to write again, as his repeated letters are a nuisance.

# Collections

Beatrix Potter wished all her paintings to be given to 'some public collection'. In accordance with that wish, much of her *oeuvre* is now concentrated in public collections.

The finished sets of watercolours for the Tales now belong to the National Trust, the Frederick Warne Archive, the British Museum Print Room and the Tate Gallery. Most of her mycological and microscope studies are in the collection of the Armitt Trust, Ambleside (Cumbria, England) and the Perth Museum and Art Gallery (Scotland). Other major collections are: the Linder Bequest (V&A), the Linder Collection (Linder Trust, on long loan to the V&A), the Free Library of Philadelphia, and the Cotsen Children's Library at Princeton University.

# Illustration Acknowledgements

The author and publishers would like to thank the following for permission to reproduce illustrations in this book: the Armitt Trust, the Beatrix Potter Society, the Cotsen Children's Library, the Free Library of Philadelphia, the National Portrait Gallery, the National Trust, the Victoria and Albert Museum, the Frederick Warne Archive and many private collectors, including Jenny Akester (page 25 *below*), John R. Cawood (page 95 *below*), the *Daily Telegraph* (page 96 *below*), Christopher Howse (page 97 *below*), Avril and Barry Miles (page 120 *below*) and John Heelis (page 147 *above*).

# Bibliography

*Beatrix Potter, 1866-1943: the Artist and her World* J. Taylor, J. I. Whalley, A. S. Hobbs and E. Battrick (London: Frederick Warne/National Trust, 1987; revised edition 1991)

*The Art of Beatrix Potter* Leslie Linder (London: Frederick Warne, 1955, revised edition 1972)

*Beatrix Potter: Artist, Storyteller, Countrywoman* Judy Taylor (London: Frederick Warne, 1986, new edition 1996, revised 2002)

*Beatrix Potter's Americans: Selected Letters* ed. Jane C. Morse (Boston: The Horn Book, 1982)

*Beatrix Potter's Art* Anne Stevenson Hobbs (London: Frederick Warne, 1989, revised edition 2004)

*Beatrix Potter's Journal* abridged Glen Cavaliero (London: Frederick Warne, 1986)

*Beatrix Potter's Letters* ed. Judy Taylor (London: Frederick Warne, revised edition 2001)

*A History of the Writings of Beatrix Potter* Leslie Linder (London: Frederick Warne, 1971, revised edition 1987)

*The Journal of Beatrix Potter from 1881 to 1897* transcr. L. Linder (London: Frederick Warne, 1966, revised edition 1989)

*So I Shall Tell you a Story: Encounters with Beatrix Potter* ed. Judy Taylor (London: Frederick Warne, 1993)

Coming in 2007:

*Beatrix Potter: A Life in Nature,* a new biography of Beatrix Potter by Linda Lear (London: Allen Lane, spring 2007)

NATURAL HISTORY INCLUDING MYCOLOGY

*Les Champignons* Introduction by Anne Stevenson Hobbs. Commentary by M. Cailleux, assisted by Mme. Roquebert (Paris: Bibliothèque de l'Image, 1996) Includes sixty-six of Beatrix Potter's fungus paintings.

*A Victorian Naturalist: Beatrix Potter's Drawings from the Armitt Collection* Eileen Jay, Mary Noble and Anne Stevenson Hobbs (London: Frederick Warne, 1992)

*Wayside and Woodland Fungi* W. P. K. Findlay (Frederick Warne, 1967) Includes fifty-nine of Beatrix Potter's fungus paintings.

CATALOGUES

*The Beatrix Potter Collection of Lloyd Cotsen* (Cotsen Occasional Press, 2004)

*Beatrix Potter: the V&A Collection* The Leslie Linder Bequest (London: V&A and Frederick Warne, 1985)

*The Linder Collection of the Watercolours and Drawings of Beatrix Potter* (London: Trustees of the Linder Collection, 1996, revised 1999)

# Index

Page references are arranged as follows: Introduction; Time Line (in *italics*); text including captions, and illustrations (**bold**). Beatrix Potter is abbreviated to 'BP', and Rupert Potter to 'RP'.


advertising 138; *see also* merchandise
Aesthetic Movement 6
agricultural shows 7, 7, **13**
*Alice's Adventures in Wonderland* 14, 59, 86, **87-8**, 88, 120, 174, **174**; *see also* Carroll, L.; Tenniel, Sir J.
Allingham, Helen 8
almanacs and calendars *13*; 30, 74, **80**, 80, 95, **95**
alphabet design 83, **83**
amphibians 8; *see also* frogs; newts; toads
animals inc. pets and livestock 8; *10-13*; 23, 59, 86, 140, 143; dead or stuffed 8, 9; 23, **28**, 29, **29**, **34-5**, 35, 67, **67**; resting or sleeping 9; **24**, **30**, **33**, **66**, 67, **82**, 83, **85**, **89**, **94**; *see also* natural history *etc.*; skulls *etc., and under names*
*Appley Dapply's Nursery Rhymes 11, 12*; 80, **80**, 118, 120-22, **120-22**
archaeological subjects 6; *10*; 57-8, **57-8**
architectural subjects *see* buildings *etc.*
Armitt, The *10*
art criticism *see* comments on art *etc.*
art education 6, 7; *10*; 59-61, 63-4, 66, 68-9, 86, 138; *see also* influences
art exhibitions and gallery visits 59, 177; *see also under names of museums and galleries*
Art Nouveau 89, 124
Art Student's Certificate (Science and Art Department) *10*; 59
artefacts 9; **31**, **33**, **36**, 57-8, **57-8**, 60, **61**, 68, **68**, **72-80**, 84, **84**, **89-94**, 93, **97-9**, **101-02**, **104**, **106-08**, **110-11**, **113**, **120-21**, **125-7**, **129**, **135-9**, **147-8**, **152**; baskets **33**, **53**, **61**, **76**, **102**, **104**, **120-21**, **128**, **131**, **171-2**; guns **53**, **89-90**, 97, **97**; umbrellas 7, **7**, **74-6**, 94, **94**, **124**, **128**, **130**; *see also* china; furniture; horses *etc.* (carts and carriages); interiors
Ashton, Sir Frederick 112
Ashyburn, nr Hawick 155
atmospheric effects, seasons, weather 8; 7, 55, **70**, 70-71, **124**, 161, **164**, 165, 173, **173**, 178; *see also* snow scenes
Auden, Wystan Hugh 100
Aulnoy, Marie Catherine de la Mothe, Comtesse d' 90
Austen, Jane 59
backgrounds *see* buildings *etc.*; interiors; landscapes *etc.*; trees *etc.*
ballet (*Tales of Beatrix Potter*) 112
Banner, Delmar H. 6, 8; 7, **7**
Banner, Josephine (Josefina de Vasconcellos) 7, 116
Barber, Charles Burton 176, **176**
Barnard, Clive 141, **141**
bats *10*; 23, 27, **27**
Battledore Ltd., Kingston NY 119
bears **36**
Bedwell Lodge, Hertfordshire 71-3, **71-3**, 119, **119**, 120-21, 156, 179
Benjamin Bouncer *see* rabbits
Bermann, Fritz (metal figurines) 181
Bewick, Thomas 35, 65
Bible, The 59
*Big Green Book, The* (Robert Graves/Maurice Sendak) 179, **179**
birds 8; *10*; **34-7**, 35, 36, 60, 65, **65**, 67, 79, **79**, 103, **103**, **134-6**; owls **128**, **135-6**, **170**, 173; poultry *11, 12*; **116-17**, 117, 119, **119**, **148**, 156, **166**, **170**; robin 104
Birnam, Perthshire *10*; 20; *see also* Heath Park
Blackburn, Jemima (née Wedderburn) 23, 35, 59, 60, 62, 65, **65**; *The Pipits* 62, 65, **65**
boats **168-71**, 169, **173**
Bolton Gardens, Kensington (No. 2) *10, 12*; 19, **19**, **70**, 70-71, 140, **146**
Bonheur, Rosa 28, 59
book design *9; 11, 12*; 92-3, 96, 97, 100, 118, 131, 135-9; covers 31, 69, **69**, 93, **93**, 96, 97, 98, 100, **101-02**, **112**, 135; endpapers 33, 98, 124, 135-9, **135-8**, **171**, 173; frontispieces 80, **80**, 104, 105, 114, 124, **125**, 139, 168; head- and tailpieces **151**, **153**, 171, **171**, 172, 173, **173**; title pages 95, **112**, **116**, 135, 139, **139**; *see also* border designs
border designs 54, **82**, 83, 86, 89, **89**, 118; *see also* book design; composition *etc.*
Borrowdale 178; Sty Head Tarn **178**
Boston, USA *12, 13*; 94
botanical subjects inc. flower paintings 6, 7, 9; *10, 11*; **9**, **44**, 45, 48, **48**, **55**, 59, 60, 62, 63, 64, **64**, 86, **93**, **104**, 114-15, **114-15**, 116, **122-4**, 124, **128**, **130-31**, 131, **133**, **135-6**, **151**, **159**; *see also* fruit and nuts; fungi *etc.*; gardens; trees *etc.*; vegetables
Brefeld, Oscar 48
Bright, John, M.P. 14, 24
British Museum (Natural History) *see* Natural History Museum
buildings, townscapes *etc.* 6, 9; **52**, 60, **61**, **70**, **74-5**, 86, **90-91**, 91, **94**, **102**, **104**, **115**, 119, **119**, **130**, **133-4**, 156, **156**, 167, **167-8**, **171-2**, 179, **179**; chimneys **134**, **156**, **167**, **171**, **179**
Bunyan, John 59
Burton, Harriet (née Leech, aunt) 8
Bush Hall, Hertfordshire 119, **119**, 179, **179**
butterflies and moths *see* insects

Caldecott, Randolph 8; 59, 92, 99, **99**, 118, 119
Cameron, Miss 59
Camfield Place, Hertfordshire *10*; 25, 38, 83, 93, 151, **151**
caricature *see* humour; self-portraits
Carr, Lucie and Kathleen 183
Carroll, Lewis 86, **87-8**, 88, 174, **174**; *Alice's Adventures in Wonderland* 14, 59, 86, **87-8**, 88, 120, 174; *see also* Tenniel, Sir J.
Carter, Annie *see* Moore, A.
Castle Cottage, Sawrey *12, 13*; 140, 147; Castle Farm *12*
Catbells, nr Keswick 51
cats and kittens 32-3, **33**, **65**, 72, **72**, 90, **90**, **93**, 96, **96**, **98-9**, **101**, 113, **113**, 119, **119**, **131**, **133-7**, 134, 137, **139**, 152, **152**, **170-71**, **173**
cattle *11, 12, 13*; 149
*Cecily Parsley's Nursery Rhymes 12*; 118, 125-9, **125-9**
ceramics *see* china
chalks and crayon 7; 156, 179; examples **28**, **156**, **179**
chickens *see* birds (poultry)
children and young people, in relation to BP 6; *10-11*; 11, 40, 43, 45, 62, 83, 84, 94, 97, 98, 100, 103, 109, 114, 116, 120, 125, 140, 170, 171, 180-83
children, drawings and portraits of 53, **53**, **176**, 177
china 9; **54**, **77-80**, **98-9**, **103**, 109, **109**, **120-23**, **125-7**, **135-6**; nursery china 181
Chorley Rubber Company (toys) 181
Choyce, Eleanor (Louie) *12, 13*
Christmas *13*; 25, 68, 76, 84, 94, 122, 125, 147, 181; cards *see* greetings card designs
Clark, Caroline, of Ulva (née Hutton) *see* Hutton, C.
clay modelling 7; 60, 141, **141**
code writing *10*; 125; *see also* Journal
Coldstream, Berwickshire (Hatchednize Wood) 50; *see also* Lennel
colour inc. use of 6, 7, 8, 9; 32, 34, 36, 43, 45, 48, 50, 54, 60, 74, 77, 80, 81, 90, 104, 121, 122, 129, 135, 136, 161-3, 165, 168; palette and pigments 7, 8; 62-3, 74, 75, 84, 144, 159, 177; *see also* 'grisaille' *etc.*

comments and opinions on art and design 6, 7, 8; 7, 20, 28, 32, 42, 59, 65, 88, 133, 140, 163, 164, 172, 178; *see also* Journal
comments on her own art 6, 7, 8; 48-9, 58, 59, 60, 66, 74, 109, 110, 122, 128, 135-6, 140, 143, 159, 170, 172, 179, 181
comments and tributes by others 6, 8, 9; 14, 31, 69, 96, 103, 116, 119, 122, 152, 157, 179, **179**, 180, **180**
commercial work 8; *10*; 19, 30, 74-80, **76**, **80**; *see also* greetings card designs; merchandise
composition and design 6, 8, 9; 14, 48, 54, 60, 61, 84, 89, 91, 92, 93, 99, 100, 104, 105, 109, 120-21, 125, 126-7, 128, 133, 137, 138, 160, 169; artistic licence 9; 72-3, 134; *see also* book design; light *etc.*; perspective *etc.*
Coniston Old Hall 156, **156**
Coniston Old Man **158**, 159
Constable, John, R.A. 7, 178, **178**
contemporary art scene, attitudes, fashion 6, 8, 9; 23, 56, 58, 59, 83, 89, 94, 167; *see also* influences
Coolidge, Henry P. *13*; 94
copying and copies 6, 8; 28, **28**, 59, 60, 65, 68, 86, 154, **154**, 178, **178**; *see also* art education; influences; parodies
copyright (registration of designs) *11, 12*; 179-81
costume inc. textiles 9; 14, 17, 19, 20, 59, 69, 74-7, **74-80**, 80, 87, **87-9**, 90, **93**, 104, 108, **108-109**, 112, **112-13**, 113, 116-17, **116-17**, 131, **131**, 178, 181, **181-2**; shoes 58, **58**, **122**; textiles and cotton trade 69, **69**, **85**, 92, **92-3**, 93, **102**; Herdwick tweed 7, **7**, **12**, **142**, 143, **146**; *see also* portfolios
Cotsen Collection, Princeton University 170
Crane, Walter 60, 118
Cruikshank, George 59

*Daily Telegraph, The* 96, 97
Dalguise House, nr Dunkeld, Perthshire *10*; **11**, 14, **15-18**, 19, 67, 112, 151
dance, as motif 8, 9; 84, **84**, **85**, 94, **95**, **96**, **108**, **119**, 137, **137**, 139
David McKay Co., publishers *see* McKay, D.
deer 8; 28, **28**, **29**, 67, **67**
Derwentwater 22, 159, 160; *see also* Fawe Park; Lingholm; 'Derwentwater Sketchbook' 52, **52**
design *see* book design; composition *etc.*
Dickens, Charles 59, 88
Dinting Vale, Glossop (calico printing works) 69
Disney, Walt *13*; 140, 181
dogs 32, 61, **61**, 97, **103**, 143, **170-73**, 171; Border terrier **22**; Duchess 130, **130**; Fly 143, **143**; Kep 141, **141-2**, 148, **148**; Pekinese *13*; **13**; Spot, **11**, 17, **17-18**
dolls *11, 12*; 69, 181-2
dormice *see under* mice
Doyle, Richard 59
drawing and draughtsmanship 6; *10*; 7, 59, 121, 140, 152; *see also* line *etc.*; style *etc.*
Drawing Societies 119, 122, 140, 157, 159
dream, as motif 31, **31**, **82**, 83, **85**
ducks *see* birds (poultry)
Duke, Stephanie (née Hyde Parker) *see* Hyde Parker, S.
*Dumpy Books for Children, The* 100
Dunkeld, Perthshire *see* Dalguise; Eastwood
Dürer, Albrecht 9

early work 6, 7, 8; *10*; 23, **28**, 35, 59-69, **61**, **64**, **66-8**, 92, 95, 156, **156**, 179, **179**; *see also* greetings card designs
ears 9; 94, **94**, 104, **104**, 110, **110-11**
Eastwood, Dunkeld, Perthshire *10*; 45
Eeswyke (formerly Lakefield), Sawrey **158**, 159
endpapers *see under* book design
Eragny Press 167
Ernest Nister, publishers *see* Nister, E.
Eskdale Show 7
Esthwaite Water **101**, **157**, 159, 161, **161**, **164**, **166**, 167
etching 7; 60, 154-5, **155**
exhibition and gallery visits *see* art exhibitions *etc.*

Fairley, Rob 23
*Fairy Caravan, The 13*; 25, 55, **55**, 100, 130, 151-4, **151-4**, 167; 'The Tale of Tuppenny' *11*
fairy tales, folk tales, fables 8; *13*; 53, **53**, 59, 60, 86, 89, 90-91, **90-91**, 117; *see also* rhymes
Falmouth, Cornwall 170
fantasy pictures 8; 55, 60, 61, **61**, 73, **73**, 81, **81-5**, 83, 84, 92, 124; *see also* fairy tales *etc.*; greetings card designs; humour; rhymes
farming *see* agricultural shows; *see also* Potter, B. (as farmer *etc.*), *and under names of animals*
Fawe Park, Keswick 47, 133, 159, **159**
ferns **53**, **133**, **142**
figure drawing *see* human subjects
fireplaces *see* interiors (hearths); light (as focus)
fish 9; 41, **41**, 43, **43**, 67, **114**, **124**
Flaxman, John 60
flower paintings *see* botanical subjects *etc.*
fossils 6; *10*; 14, 41, 56, **56**
Foster, Myles Birket 6
Foster, Vere Henry Lewis 60
foxes 9; **89**, **101**, **154**, **166**, 167
Frederick Warne, publishers *see* Warne, F.
freshwater creature 38, **39**
'Frog he would a-fishing go, A' *10*; 74, 92
frogs 42, **42-3**, 99, **99**, **101**, **114-15**, 115, 124, **124**; *see also* 'Frog he would a-fishing go, A'
fruit and nuts 30, **52**, 54, **94**, **125-8**, **177**; pine-cone 45, **45**
fungi, lichens, mosses 6, 7, 9; *10, 11*; 14, 23, 40, 41, 45, 48-51, **48-51**, 53-5, **53-5**, 56, 59, 115
furniture 9; **82**, **92-3**, 93, **95**, **105**, **109-11**, **125**, **132**, 133, **148**; *see also* interiors

*Game of Peter Rabbit, The 11*; 181
gardens 45, 47, **104**, 128, **133**, 151, **151**, **158-9**, 159, **177**
Garland, Nicholas 96, 97, **96-7**
Gaskell, Elizabeth 14
Gaskell, Rev. William 14; photograph of **15**
geology 56, 154
Germany *12*; 182
*Ginger and Pickles 12*; **102**, 130, 138, **138**
Gloucester 91; *see also* Harescombe Grange; *Tailor of Gloucester, The*
Gould, John 35
governesses *10*; 59; *see also* Cameron, Miss; Moore (née Carter), A.
Grahame, Kenneth 42
Graves, Robert 179
Greenaway, Kate 59
Greene, Graham 100
greetings card designs 8; *10*; 19, 30, **30**, 61, 68, 74-80, **74-80**, 96, 103, 119, 120-21, 140, 147
Grimshaw, Atkinson 71
'grisaille' and grey wash, use of 7; 81, 91; examples **29**, **53**, **71-3**, **81**, **91**
guinea pigs 74, 77-8, **77-9**, **91**, 92; *see also* 'Tale of Tuppenny, The'

handkerchiefs *12*; 181
*Hanne Nüte un de lütte Pudel* (Fritz Reuter/Otto Speckter) 117, **117**
*Happy Pair, A* (Frederic E. Weatherly) *10*; 76, **76**, 92
hares *see under* rabbits
Harescombe Grange, Stroud, Glos. *10*; 53
Harris, Joel Chandler 89, **89**
Harvey, Michael 14

Hastings, Sussex *11*; 171
Hawkshead, Lancashire *12*
Heath Park, Birnam, Perthshire 20, **21**
hedgehogs 8; 122, **122**; Mrs. Tiggy-winkle 112, **112**
Heelis family 147
Heelis, Helen Beatrix (née Potter) *see* Potter, B.
Heelis, William *12, 13*; 12, 20, 97; photograph of 146, **146**
Herdwick Sheep Breeders' Association *13*; *see also* sheep (Herdwicks)
Herring, W. A. 130
Hertfordshire 90; *see also* Bedwell Lodge; Bush Hall; Camfield Place
Hildesheimer & Faulkner *10*; 30, 74-8, **76**, **78-9**
Hill Top (Farm), Sawrey *11, 12, 13*; **11-12**, 126-7, **126-7**, 134, **134**, 140, 147, **147**, 148, 179, 180, **180**
Hogarth, William 8
Holehird, Windermere 48
*Horn Book (Magazine), The 12, 13*; 45, 66, 177
horses and ponies **36**, **61**, 143, 153, **153**, **157**, **171**, **173**; carts and carriages *13*; **61**, **153**, **157**, **171**, **173**
human subjects 8; 14, 49, 52, **52-3**, 53, 86, 88, **97**, 103, **103-04**, 104, **109**, 150, **175**; faces **61**, 103, **103**, 150, **150**; *see also* self-portraits
humming birds 60
humour 8, 9; 14, 37, 54, 60, 61, 74, 79, 82-5, **82-5**, 89, **89**, 96-9, **96-9**, 108, **108**, 118, 140, 148, 173; caricature 8, 54, **54**, 61, **61**, 74, **74**; *see also* greetings card designs; Journal; parodies; self-portraits
Hunt and Roskell, silversmiths 68
Hunt, William Henry 'Bird's Nest' 6; 43
Hutton, Caroline (later Clark, of Ulva, cousin) *10*; 20, 122, 146
Hyde Parker, Stephanie (later Duke, cousin) 114, 128

Ilfracombe, Devon 170, 171
illustrations to others *10, 13*; 17, 26, 59, 60, 74, **74-6**, 76, 78, 86-92, **87-91**, 124, **124**, **170**, 173, **173**, 174; *see also* natural history *etc.*; rhymes
influences, artistic 6, 8, 9; *10*; 23, 59, 60, 69, 89, 92, 99, 100, 117, 118, 119, 124, 173, 174, 176, 178; *see also under artists and styles*; literary *10*; 25, 59, 88, 100, 124
ink drawings *see* line *etc.*
insects 8; *10, 11*; 23, 38, 40, 43, 68, 91, 92, 114, **115**; bee 43, **43**; butterflies and moths *10, 11*; 38, **38**, 40, 60, 68, **68**
interiors 9; 26, 27, **27**, **69**, 71-3, **71-3**, **77-9**, **82**, **87-8**, **92-5**, 103, **103-11**, 110, 120-21, **120-21**, **125-7**, 131, **131**, **148**, 152, **152**; hearths **94**, **104**, **106-07**, **109**, **125**, 152, **152**; *see also* furniture
Invalid Children's Aid Association (ICAA) 74
Isherwood, Christopher 100

Japanese style 89
Jemima Puddle-Duck doll *12*; 69, 182
*Jemima Puddle-Duck's Painting Book 12*; 116, **116**
Journal inc. excerpts 6, 8, 9; *10, 11*; 16, 24, 28, 29, 32, 36, 40, 41, 48-9, 50, 58, 59, 60, 68, 69, 74, 79, 130, 133, 151, 163, 165

Kauffmann, Maria Anna Angelica 59
Kensington, London *10, 12*; **69**; National Art Training School 59; *see also* Bolton Gardens; *and under names of museums*
Kep *see* dogs
Keswick, Cumberland *see* Derwentwater; Fawe Park; Lingholm; Newlands; Keswick Market 51, 52, **52**; Keswick Show 7, **7**
Kew (Royal Botanic Gardens) *11*
King, Charles G. Y. **142**, 143

Lake District 6, 9; *10, 11*; 133, 140, 151, 156, 178, 180, **180**; *see also under names of places*
Lakefield, Sawrey *see* Eeswyke; Lakefield Cottage 131, **131**
landscapes 6, 8, 9; 14, 60, 61, **61**, **81**, 86, 90, **101-02**, 116, **116**, **128**, **134**, 147, **147**, 154-5, **154-5**, 157, **157-8**, **160-66**, 161, 178, **178**; snow scenes 8; **80**, **90**, **94**, 164-5, **164-5**; *see also* gardens; seascapes; trees *etc.*
Landseer, Sir Edwin, R.A. 28, **28**
late work 8; 74, 80, 95, **95**, 140-41, **141**, 143-5, **143-5**, 147-54, **147-54**, 161, **161-9**, 163-5, 167-74, **171-3**, **175**, 177, **177**
Lear, Edward 8; 59, 86, 118, 173; 'The Owl and the Pussy Cat' 92, **170**, 173, **173**
Leech, Harriet *see* Burton, H. (née Leech)
Leech, Helen *see* Potter, H. (née Leech)
Leech, John, artist 59
Leigh Smith, Bernard 24
Lennel, Coldstream, Berwickshire 10
lichens *see* fungi
light and shade 8, 9; 7, 45, 46, 72-3, **72-3**, 161, 164; light as focus 9; **31**, **84**, **87-8**, **92-3**, **94**, **106-07**, **109**, **125**, **129**, **147**, **152**; moonlight 8, 9; 91, **91**, **128**, 153, **153**
Linder, Leslie 16, 112; Linder Bequest (V&A Museum) *10*; 76, 136, 147; Linder Collection (Linder Trust) *10*
Lindeth How, Windermere *12*
line (drawing) 7, 8; 26, 45, 62, 76, 92, 104, 116, 124, 131, 135, 152, 167, 171, 172, 174; examples **24**, **26**, **30-31**, **36**, **40**, **42**, **52**, **54-5**, **61**, **65**, **77**, **82-3**, **89**, **93**, **99**, **103-05**, **112**, **114-17**, **119**, **130-32**, **136**, **143**, **145**, **148-56**, **166**, **170-74**, **179**; *see also* chalks *etc.*; drawing *etc.*; media *etc.*
Lingholm, Keswick 22, **22**, 55, 160
Linnean Society of London *11*; 48
lino cuts 60
literature 59, 60, 86ff, 100, 140; *see also* fairy tales *etc.*; illustrations *etc.*; influences; rhymes
lithographs and lithography 8; *10-11*; 28, 40, 74-5, 76; examples **40**, **74**, **76**, **78**
Liverpool *13*
lizards 23, 42
Lockhart, James G. 25
London 6; 23, 56, 151, 157, 182; City (Bucklersbury) *10*; 57-8; *see also* Bolton Gardens; Kensington; Kew; Natural History Museum; Royal Academy of Arts; Tate Gallery; Victoria and Albert Museum; Zoological Gardens
Lyme Regis, Dorset 171, **172**

Macdonald, Kitty (Katie) 112
McIntosh, Charles *10*; 48, 49
McKay, Alexander (Philadelphia) 171, 172
McKay, David, Co., publishers (Philadelphia) *13*; 151, 170ff
McKay, Margery 171
Mackenzie, A. F., of Birnam, photographer 20, **20**
Mahony, Bertha *see* Miller, Bertha Mahony
Mallet, Richard (cousin) 84
Manchester 69
Martineau, Caroline *10-11*; 40
Massee, George *11*
'mechanicals' *see* toy pictures
media used 7, 8; 26, 60, 62; *see also* support *etc.*, *and under names of media*
Melford Hall, Suffolk 128
merchandise *11, 12*; 181-2, **181-2**; *see also* advertising
Merritt, Anna Lea 176, **176**
mice and dormice 8, 9; 23, 25, **25**, 30, 31, **31**, 43, **43**, 65, **65**, 72, 73, **73**, 83, **83**, **91-3**, 92-3, 95, 96, **95-6**, 108, 109, **108-09**, 110, **110-11**,

120-21, **120-22**, 122, 125, **129**, **135-6**, 138, **138**, **177**; Xarifa (dormouse) 24, **24-5**, 25, 26, 67
microscope studies 7, 8; *10, 11*; 23, 38, **38-40**, 40, 68, 140
Millais, Sir John Everett, P. R. A. 14, 20, 24, 69; photograph of **69**
Miller, Bertha Mahony 109, 110
Milne, Alan Alexander 140
miniature letters 183, **183**
mole **91**
Monk Coniston Estate *13*
moonlight *see under* light *etc.*
Moore family *10, 11*; 80
Moore, Alan 180
Moore, Anne Carroll *12*; photograph of **12**
Moore, Annie (née Carter) *10*; 80, 104
Moore, Edwin *10*
Moore, Eric *10*; 170
Moore, Noël Christian *10, 13*; 11, 104, 125; photograph of **11**
Moore, Norah *11*
mosses *see* fungi
movement, sense of 8, 9; 32, **32**, 98-9, **99**, 110, **110**, 121, 136, 137
museums 23, 26; *see also under names*
music books 181

narrative art 9; 65, 74, 81, 89, 92-9, **92-9**, 100, 180, **180**; *see also* picture letters *etc.*
National Art Training School *see under* Kensington
National Trust, The *10, 12, 13*; 122, 144, 160, 177
natural history illustration 6, 7, 8, 9; *10, 11*; 23, **24-51**, 60, **64**, **66-8**, **80ff**, 83, 94, **94-5**, **124**, **143ff**; *see also* Potter, B. (as naturalist *etc.*), *and under subjects*
Natural History Museum, South Kensington 23, 29, 40
Near Sawrey *see* Sawrey
Newlands, nr Keswick **155**
newts 23, 42, 114, **115**
Nister, Ernest, publishers *10*; 74, 79, 90, 96
nursery china (Grimwades) 181
nursery rhymes *see* rhymes
Nursing Trust *12*

oils 59, 155; examples **7**, **176**
onions *see* vegetables
opinions on art *see* comments *etc.*
*Our Dear Relations* (Frederic E. Weatherly) 78
'Owl and the Pussy Cat, The' 92, **170**, 173, **173**
owls *see under* birds

paintbox 62-4, **62**
painting *see* art education; art exhibitions *etc.*; oils; watercolour
painting books *12*; 62, 116, **116**, 181
palette *see under* colour *etc.*
panoramic books *11, 12*; 92, 95-9, **95-9**, 100
Parker, Audrey 152
Parker, Peter 100
parodies 8; 84, **106-07**, 107, 117, 174, **175**, 176-7, **177**; *see also* copying *etc.*; humour
Parton family 53, **53**
Pasteur, Louis 48
pen-and-ink drawings *see* line *etc.*
pencil drawings *see* line *etc.*
people, drawings of *see* human subjects
Perrault, Charles 53
Perry, Marian Frazer Harris 172
perspective and depth 8, 9; *10*; 59, 71-3, 87-8, 124; *see also* composition *etc.*; scale *etc.*
Perth Museum and Art Gallery *10*
Perthshire, Scotland 61; *see also* Birnam; Dalguise House; Dunkeld; Eastwood; Heath Park; Perth Museum and Art Gallery; Tay (River);
'Perthshire Naturalist' *see* McIntosh, C.
Peter Piper *see* rabbits
'Peter Rabbit Books, The' *see under* Potter, B., *and under titles*
Peter Rabbit doll *11*; 181, **181**; Steiff doll 182, **182**
*Peter Rabbit's Almanac for 1929 13*; 80, **80**, 95, **95**
*Peter Rabbit's Painting Book 12*; 62
pets *see* animals; *see also under names*
'Phiz' (Hablot Knight Browne) 59
photographs and photography 14, 16, 17, 19, 20, 67, 94; BP and 7; 14, 53, 56, 60, 171; RP and 14, 19, 20, 67, 94, 146; examples inc. portraits **10-22**, **25**, **69**, **142**, **146**; *see also* King, C. G. Y.; Mackenzie, A. F.; Potter, R.
picture letters and stories 8; *10, 11*; 45, 52, 92, 100, 104, 109, 170, **170**, 173; *see also* narrative art
Picturesque, The 9
*Pie and the Patty-Pan, The 11*; 36, **36**, 96, **101**, 130-31, **130-31**, **135-6**
pigs *11, 12*; 55, **55**, **102**, **119**, **128**, 141, 147-9, **147-9**, **171-2**, **175**
*Pipits, The* (Jemima Blackburn) 62, 65, **65**
Pissarro, Lucien 167
place-card 68, **68**
plants, flowering *see* botanical subjects *etc.*; *see also* fungi *etc.*; trees *etc.*
plaques 60, 141
portfolios (fabric) 50, 69, 80, 122
portraits *see* children, ... portraits of; human subjects (faces); photographs *etc.*; self-portraits
Potter family *10, 11*; 22, 41, 59, 68, 71, 159
Potter, Beatrix (later Heelis)
**as artist**: art works *see under media and subjects*; exhibited, given away or sold 120, 140, 177; preserved *13*; *see also* portfolios; reproduced 8; *see also* art education; Art Student's Certificate; comments *etc.*; commercial work; humour; media *etc.*; photographs *etc.*; signatures *etc.*; style *etc.*; working methods
**biographical details** 6; *10-13*; 14, 17, 19, 20, 22, 23, 25, 59, 60, 68, 83, 100, 140, 144, 146-7, 150, 151, 182; education *10*; 59; eyesight 8; 80, 140; illness *10, 13*; 25
**photographs of 10-22**, **25**, **142**, 143, 146, **146**
**portrait of** 7, **7**; *see also* self-portraits
**as benefactor** *12*; 74, 80, 140, 144, 177
**as businesswoman** 74-80, 140, 181-2
**as collector and conservationist** 8, 9; *12, 13*; 133, 140, 144, 177
**as farmer, landowner and countrywoman** *11, 12, 13; 7*, 45, 80, 97, 140, 143, 144, 147, 148, 149, 164, 171; *see also* animals *etc.*; Hill Top (Farm)
**as naturalist and scientist** 6, 7, 8; *10, 11*; 23, 27, 35, 36, 38, 40, 41, 46, 48, 54, 55, 60, 64, 83, 94, 140; *see also* animals *etc.*; botanical subjects *etc.*; natural history *etc.*
**as political campaigner** *12*; 97, 182
**as writer: books, general** 6, 8, 9; *11-13*; 14, 23, 36, 55, 62, 69, 72, 76, 89, 98, 100ff, 103, 109, 118ff, 133, 135, 138, 140, 143, 170, 183; Braille editions *12, 13*; translations *12*; *see also* advertising; book design; Journal; merchandise; music books; painting books; panoramic books; Peter Rabbit's Almanac *etc.*
**books, by title**
*Appley Dapply's Nursery Rhymes 11, 12*; 80, **80**, 118, 120-22, **120-22**
*Cecily Parsley's Nursery Rhymes 12*; 118, 125-9, **125-9**
*Fairy Caravan, The 13*; 25, 55, **55**, 100, 130, 151-4, **151-4**, 167
*Ginger and Pickles 12*; **102**, 130, 138, **138**
*Pie and the Patty-Pan, The 11*; 36, **36**, 96, **101**, 130-31, **130-31**, **135-6**
*Roly-Poly Pudding, The (The Tale of Samuel Whiskers) 12*; 84, 130, 133-4, **133-4**, 137-9, **137**, **139**, 148
*Sister Anne 13*

*Sly Old Cat, The* 92, 98-9, **98-9**
*Story of A Fierce Bad Rabbit, The* *11, 12*; 97, **97**
*Story of Miss Moppet, The* *11, 12*; 95-6, **95-6**, 97
*Tailor of Gloucester, The* 8; *11*; 31, 53, 69, 76, 92-3, **102**, 108-09, **108-09**, 135, **135-6**, 136, 178
*Tale of Benjamin Bunny, The* *11, 12*; 32-3, **33**, 47, **102**, 104, 125, 128, 159
*Tale of Jemima Puddle-Duck, The* 8; *11*; **116**, 116-17, 141
*Tale of Johnny Town-Mouse, The* *12*
*Tale of Little Pig Robinson, The* *13*; 100, 167, 168, 170-75, **170-73**, **175**
*Tale of Mr. Jeremy Fisher, The* *10, 11*; 43, **43**, 48, 61, **101**, 114-15, **114-15**, 124
*Tale of Mr. Tod, The* *12*; 89, 100, **101**, 135, **166**, 167
*Tale of Mrs. Tiggy-Winkle, The* *11*; 112, **112**, 183
*Tale of Mrs. Tittlemouse, The* 8; *12*; 38, 43, **43**
*Tale of Peter Rabbit, The* 8; *11, 12, 13*; 11, 30, 45, 49, 72, 89, **101**, 103-07, **103-07**, 113, 118, 125, 135, **135-6**, 139, 140, 141, 176-7, **176-7**, 181-2
*Tale of Pigling Bland, The* *12*; **102**, 128, 130, 147-8, **147-8**
*Tale of Samuel Whiskers, The see* Roly-Poly Pudding, The
*Tale of Squirrel Nutkin, The* *11*; 22, 32, 43, 55, **55**, 69, **69**, 135, **135-6**, 139, 160, 183
*Tale of The Flopsy Bunnies, The* *12*
*Tale of Timmy Tiptoes, The* *12*
*Tale of Tom Kitten, The* *11*; 113, **113**
*Tale of Two Bad Mice, The* *8*; *11*; 110-11, **110-11**, 139
*Wag-by-Wall* *13*
**letters inc. excerpts** 6, 7, 8; *11, 13*; 7, 33, 42, 45, 62, 86, 88, 96, 109, 110, 118, 119, 122, 128, 134, 135-6, 140, 143, 147, 148, 149, 151, 152, 153, 159, 164, 171, 172, 173, 178, 182; *see also* miniature letters; picture letters
**literary manuscripts and unpublished writings** 43, **43**, 62, 63, **63**, 64, 95, 97, **97**, 98-9, **98-9**, 108, 118, 148, 171; 'Book of Rhymes' *11*; 118, 119, 122, 125; 'The Tale of Tuppenny' *11* *see also* children and young people *etc.*; comments *etc.*; Journal; humour; quotations *etc.*
Potter, Bertram (brother) 6; *10-12*; 20, 23, 38, 59, 60, 61, 103, 154-5, **155**; photographs of **11**, **21**; Mrs. Bertram (née Mary Welsh Scott) *11*; 155
Potter, Edmund, M.P., F.R.S. (grandfather) *10*; 14, 69, 83, 93, 151
Potter, Helen (née Leech, mother) *10-13*; 59, 140, 150, **150**; photograph of **11**
Potter, Helen Beatrix *see* Potter, B.
Potter, Jessy (née Crompton, grandmother) *10*; 14, 83, 93, 151
Potter, Rupert (father) *10-12*; 14, 19, 20, 59, 67, 140; sketchbook 117; photography and 14, 19, 20, 67, 94, 146; photographs of **11**, **21**; photographs by **10-11**, 14, 16, 18, 20, **14-22**, **25**, 67, **69**, 94, **146**
Potter, Walter Bertram (brother) *see* Potter, Bertram
poultry *see under* birds
Pre-Raphaelites 7-8
printing and book production 60, 74, 100, 135, 136; *see also* book design; composition *etc.*
*Punch* 59

quotations from BP 6, 7, 8, 9; *10, 11, 13*; 7, 14, 19, 23-5, 28-30, **29**, **32**, 33, 40-42, **42**, **45**, 48, **49**, 50, 56, **58**, 59, **60**, 62, 65, **66**, 68-9, 74, 79, **86**, 88, 96, 103-04, **103**, 108, **109-10**, 112-13, 116-17, **118**, 119, 122, 128, **130**, 133-5, **136**, 140, 143, **143**, 147-9, 151-3, **151**, 159, **159**, 163-4, 165, 170-74, **172**, 177-9, 181-2

rabbit toys *see* dolls
rabbits and hares 6, 8; *13*; 23, 25, 61, **61**, 66, **66**, 67, 74-5, **74-6**, 80, **80**, **82-3**, 83, **87-9**, **91**, 94, 95, **94-5**, 97, **97**, **101-07**, 103, 112, 125, **125-7**, 127, **135-6**, **177**; Benjamin Bouncer (Benjamin Bunny) *10*; 19, **19**, 74, 76, **76**; Peter Piper (Peter Rabbit) *10, 11*; 30, **30**, **82**, 83, 87, **87-9**, 89
'Rabbits' Christmas Party, The' 94, **94**, 95
Ransome, Arthur 140
rats **91**, **98-9**, 108, **108**, **133**, **137**, 137-9, **139**; Sammy 84, **85**
Rawnsley, Canon Hardwicke D. *10, 11, 12*
Renoir, Pierre Auguste 94
reptiles 8; *see also* lizards
Reuter, Fritz 117
rhymes 8; *11, 12*; 54, 60, 86, 92, **92-3**, 95, 99, **99**, 100, 103, 118-22, **119-22**, 124-9, **124-9**, 160
Richter, Adrian Ludwig 86
*Roly-Poly Pudding, The (The Tale of Samuel Whiskers)* *12*; 84, 130, 133-4, **133-4**, 137-9, **137**, **139**, 148
Roscoe, Sir Henry, F.R.S. (uncle) *11*; 31, 34, 48, 84, 94
Roscoe, Lucy (Lady Roscoe, née Potter, aunt) 94
Royal Academy of Arts 176
Runciman, Sir Steven 100
Ruskin, John 8; 23
Sawrey, Lancashire *11, 12, 13*; 130-31, **130-31**, 133-4, **133-4**, 140, **142**, 147, **147**, 153, 159, 161ff, **180**; *see also* Castle Cottage; Eeswyke; Esthwaite Water; Hill Top (Farm); Lakefield Cottage
scale and format 7, 8, 9; 57, 100, 110, 115, 131, 135, 138, 139, 167; *see also* book design; composition *etc.*; perspective *etc.*
Science and Art Department, South Kensington *see* Art Student's Certificate
scientific work *see* natural history *etc.*; Potter, B. (as naturalist and scientist)
Scotland 6; *10*; 14, 19, 50; *see also under names of places*
Scott, Sir Walter 60
sculptural quality 6, 7, 9; 25, 45, 54, 58, 81, 169; *see also* 'grisaille' *etc.*
sea anemone **41**
seascapes **168-9**, 170, **171**, **173**
self-portraits 103, 148, **148-9**, 149
Sendak, Maurice 6; 179, **179**
'sepia', use of 8; 47, 119, 131, 136, 167; examples **47**, **54**, **98-9**, **119**, **122**, **130-34**, **137**, **147-8**, **158**, **160**, **166**, **177**
Seuss, Dr. 140
Shakespeare, William *10*; 59, 124
sheep 8; *11, 13*; **116**, 140, 143-4, **144-5**, 147, **173-5**, 174; Herdwicks *11, 13*; **13**, 144, **144-5**, 151; Herdwick tweed *see under* costume; *see also* agricultural shows
shrew 92
Sidmouth, Devon 171
signatures and monograms **31**, **40**, **53**, **57-8**, 60, **61**, **71**, **73**, 74, **75-7**, 80, **80-81**, **83**, **87**, **89-90**, **92-4**, **120-21**, **125-6**, **128**, **149**, **156**, 177, **177**
*Sister Anne* *13*
sketchbooks and sketching 6, 8; *10*; 32, **32**, 36, **36**, 52, 60, 61, **61**, 66, 117, 140, **150**, **159**, 160, **161ff**, 163, 166, *and passim*; 'Derwentwater Sketchbook' 52, **52**
skulls and skeletons 8; 26, **26**, 27
sleep, as motif *see* animals (resting or sleeping); dream, as motif
*Sly Old Cat, The* 92, 98-9, **98-9**
Smailholm, Roxburghshire 49
Smithson, Alison 9
snails 8; 23, 124
snow scenes *see under* landscapes
South Kensington, London *see* Kensington
South Kensington Museum *see* Victoria and Albert Museum
Speckter, Otto 8; 86, 117, **117**
spiders 7, 8; *11*; 23, 38, **39-40**, 40, 43, 55, **55**
Spot *see* dogs
Squire, Tom H. 57-8

squirrels 30, **30**, 32, **32**, 55, **55**, 81, **81**, **135-6**, 160, **160**
Steer, Philip Wilson 8
Stephens, Arthur L. 136
still life 68, **68**, 122, **123**, 138
Storey, Tom *12, 13*; photograph of **13**
*Story of A Fierce Bad Rabbit, The 11, 12*; 97, **97**
*Story of Miss Moppet, The 11, 12*; 95-6, **95-6**, 97
Sturges, Katharine *13*
*Sty Head Tarn, Borrowdale* (John Constable) **178**
style and technique 6, 7, 8, 9; 14, 23, 25, 34, 36, 37, 38, 48, 49, 51, 56, 58, 60, 66, 74, 80, 81, 86, 121, 128, 160, 167, 168, 177; *see also* colour *etc.*; composition *etc.* ; media *etc.*; photographs *etc.*; support *etc.*; working methods
Sullivan, Edmund Joseph 153
*Sunday Herald, The* 149
support (paper, board *etc.*) 32, 40, 68, 71, 75, 78, 91, 103, 122, 125, 126; *see also* media *etc.*

*Tailor of Gloucester, The* 8; *11*; 31, 53, 69, 76, 92-3, **102**, 108-09, **108-09**, 135, **135-6**, 136, 178
Talbot, Bryan 180, **180**
*Tale of Benjamin Bunny, The 11, 12*; 32-3, **33**, 47, **102**, 104, 125, 128, 159
*Tale of Jemima Puddle-Duck, The* 8; *11*; **116**, 116-17, 141
*Tale of Johnny Town-Mouse, The 12*
*Tale of Little Black Sambo, The* (Helen Bannerman) 100
*Tale of Little Pig Robinson, The 13*; 100, 167, 168, 170-75, **170-73**, **175**
*Tale of Mr. Jeremy Fisher, The 10, 11*; 43, **43**, 48, 61, **101**, 114-15, **114-15**, 124
*Tale of Mr. Tod, The 12*; 89, 100, **101**, 135, **166**, 167
*Tale of Mrs. Tiggy-Winkle, The 11*; 112, **112**, 183
*Tale of Mrs. Tittlemouse, The* 8; *12*; 38, 43, **43**
*Tale of One Bad Rat, The* (Bryan Talbot) 180, **180**
*Tale of Peter Rabbit, The* 8; *11, 12, 13*; 11, 30, 45, 49, 72, 89, **101**, 103-07, **103-07**, 113, 118, 125, 135, **135-6**, 139, 140, 141, 176-7, **176-7**, 181-2
*Tale of Pigling Bland, The 12*; **102**, 128, 130, 147-8, **147-8**
*Tale of Samuel Whiskers, The see* Roly-Poly Pudding, The
*Tale of Squirrel Nutkin, The 11*; 22, 32, 43, 55, **55**, 69, **69**, 135, **135-6**, 139, 160, 183
*Tale of The Flopsy Bunnies, The 12*
*Tale of Timmy Tiptoes, The 12*
*Tale of Tom Kitten, The 11*; 113, **113**
'Tale of Tuppenny, The' *11*
*Tale of Two Bad Mice, The* 8; *11*; 110-11, **110-11**, 139
Tate Gallery 120
Tay (River), Perthshire 45, 61; *see also* Eastwood
technique *see* style *etc.*
Teignmouth, Devon **167-9**, 168, 171
*Temple Shakespeare, The* 100
Tenniel, Sir John 8; 14, 88, 174, **174**
textiles *see under* costume
Thiselton-Dyer, Sir William *11*
Thompson, Bruce *13*
Thorburn, Archibald 35
'Three Little Mice, The' 92-3, **92-3**, 118
tiles 60, 181
toads 42, 54, **54-5**, 55, 118
tortoise 114, **115**
'toy pictures' 83, 129
toys *see* dolls; 'toy pictures'
transfer printing 7; 60, 62
trees, woodland *etc.* 6; 30, **30**, 54, **55**, 60, 61, **61**, **81**, 89, **89**, **90**, **116**, **119**, **128**, **133**, 151, **151**, **153**, **157-60**, 160, **162-3**, **166**, **173**; leaves 9; **40**, 46, **46**, **84**, 90, **90**; pine-cone 45, **45**; *see also* botanical subjects *etc.*; fungi *etc.*; gardens; landscapes *etc.*
tributes *see* comments and tributes *etc.*
Troutbeck, Westmorland 56, 97, **154-5**, 155; Troutbeck Park Farm *12, 13*
Turner, Joseph Mallord William, R.A. 8; 59

umbrellas *see under* artefacts
*Uncle Remus* (Joel Chandler Harris) 17, 83, 86, 89, **89**
United States of America *13*; 94; *see also* Battledore Ltd.; Boston, USA; Coolidge, H. P.; Cotsen Collection; *Horn Book (Magazine), The*; King, C. G. Y.; McKay *etc.*; Miller, B. M.; Moore, A. C.; Perry, M. F. H.

variant and unused designs 25, **25**, 30, **30**, 72, **72**, 74, **74-6**, 80, **80**, **82**, 83, **87-8**, 89, 91, **91**, 92-3, **92-3**, 95, **95**, 98, **98-9**, 100, 103, **103-110**, 104-05, 107, 108, 109, 110, 112, **112**, 118, 119, **119-22**, 120-21, 122, 125, **125-31**, 126-7, 128, 129, 130-31, 134, **134**, **147**, 148, **148**, 173, **173**, 177, **177**
Vasconcellos, Josefina de *see* Banner, J.
Vaughan, Sir James 33
vegetables **52**, **94**, **103**, **128**; onions 9; 47, **47**
Victoria and Albert Museum, South Kensington 76, 118, 178, 183; Linder Bequest 10; 76, 136, 147

*Wag-by-Wall 13*
Walker, Frederick 6
wallpaper (Peter Rabbit) *11*; 181
Warne, Frederick, publishers *11-13*; 30, 43, 98, 100ff, 103, 104, 105, 108, 127, 130, 135, 140, 151, 171, 181
Warne, Fruing 143, 149, 159
Warne, Harold *12*; 97, 98
Warne, Louie 97
Warne, Nellie 43, 98
Warne, Norman *11*; 7, 86, 103, 118, 131
watercolour inc. examples 6, 7, 8, 9, 55, 59, 62, 64, 66, 71, 74, 77, 81, 100, 103, 104, 152, 165, 167, 174; examples **9**, **25**, **27**, **29-39**, **41**, **43-58**, **64**, **66-8**, **70-73**, **75-6**, **79-80**, **84-5**, **87-8**, **90-99**, **103**, **106-116**, **120-29**, **133-5**, **137-9**, **144**, **147-8**, **157-69**, **175**, **177-8**; *see also* 'grisaille' *etc.*
Waterford, Louisa, Marchioness of 59
Watling, Roy 48
weather *see* atmospheric effects *etc.*
Weatherly, Frederic E. *10*; 76; *A Happy Pair 10*; 75, 76, **76**, 92; *Our Dear Relations* 78
Webb, Beatrice (née Potter) 149
Weir, Harrison William 35
Weymouth, Dorset 41
Whistler, James Abbott McNeill 71
Wight, Mrs. M. E. 42
Windermere and area 8; *12*; 96, 177; *see also* Holehird; Lindeth How; Troutbeck
wolves **26**, **53**
women artists 59, 74
Woodcote, West Horsley, Surrey 34
working methods 6, 7, 9; 48, 53, 92, 112, 114, 125, 127, 131, 135, 161, 163; *see also* photographs *etc.*; style *etc.*
World Wars *12, 13*
Wray, Windermere *12*; Wray Castle *10*

Xarifa (dormouse) 24, **24-5**, 25, 26, 67

Zoological Gardens, London 23, 36